William M. Blackburn

The Rebel Prince

or, Lessons from the career of the young man Absalom

William M. Blackburn

The Rebel Prince
or, Lessons from the career of the young man Absalom

ISBN/EAN: 9783337951016

Printed in Europe, USA, Canada, Australia, Japan

Cover: Foto ©Lupo / pixelio.de

More available books at **www.hansebooks.com**

THE REBEL PRINCE,

OR

LESSONS FROM THE CAREER

OF

THE YOUNG MAN ABSALOM.

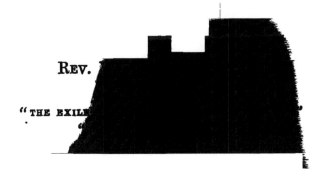

Rev.

"THE EXIL

CONTENTS.

PREFACE.

THIS volume has grown out of a series of lectures, most of which were delivered to two different congregations. While some of the original branches have been pruned away, others have been added by growth and graft. The tree must now be judged by its fruits.

The record of Absalom's life in 2 Samuel xiii.—xix. is as clear and concise as if written by the court-prophet Nathan. It has no parallel to it in Chronicles, and stands alone as a graphic piece of inspired Hebrew literature. In one view it is a vivid biography of the young man Absalom, the prodigal son of the Old Testament, who perished in his sins. In another view it is a sacred tragedy, full of most striking pictures of human nature, varied with deeply laid plots, enriched by frequent changes of scene, and enlivened by a great diversity of characters. For the study of the motives, policies, principles, and characters of evil and designing men, there are few portions of Scripture more profitable. Rarely do seven chapters furnish such a group of bold actors, such a record of great crimes against God

1 *   5

and men, and such signal divine judgments upon the
wicked. In the Prince Absalom we see the accomplished
demagogue and the ambitious politician; in Ahithophel
the wise but corrupt statesman; in Amnon, Jonadab, and
Shimei, three "lewd fellows of the baser sort;" in Ziba
the shrewdness of an experienced swindler; in Joab the
deepest private revenge combined with an effective use of
his great military talents for eminent public services, and
these are abundantly able to supply all the dark deeds required in a vigorous, thrilling drama. Better men also
appear, and it is worthy of notice that they are all upon
the side of King David, who is the chief personage in the
record. The priests—the church—did not abandon him in
the time of his greatest national troubles. Unscrupulous
as Joab was, his loyalty, during Absalom's rebellion, was
worthy of the greatest general under the Hebrew monarchy.
Hushai gave his eloquence to the holy cause. Ittai was
heroic in his patriotism, and poor Prince Mephibosheth,
had he not been lame, might have carried his true allegiance into kindly rivalry with that of Barzillai and his
neighbouring chieftains of Gilead.

Not a good, moral, godly man is named among those
who engaged in Absalom's rebellion, unless the silence
concerning the character of the incompetent Amasa is to
be interpreted in his favour. The Prince seemed to depend upon a general ungodliness and hatred of David's
piety then prevalent in the nation. The men, their spirit,
their crafty designs, and their bold methods of gaining
their ends, all tended to a great tragedy.

In a third view we have before us a solemn history. It

presents us the record of a desperate attempt to dethrone David, revolutionize the nation, and destroy the theocracy. It is the chief one of all the movements which finally resulted in the separation of the ten tribes from the federal government. Absalom prepared the way for Jeroboam. No reader will fail to notice the hand of God in all this inspired history. He sustained his servant David in all his royal trials, and preserved the throne, the church, and the city of the great king, by a series of remarkable providences.

Nor do these three views exhaust the record. It is a striking picture of a family, deserving of close and frequent study. A father's sins are intensified in some of his children, and bring the sword into his own house. There are shown to us some of the plainest lessons upon family government, family trials, and family judgments. It is not only as a king that David is sorely afflicted, but as a father. Those who magnify his faults should justly remember his very great and very many trials. In no other part of his reign did he exhibit more wisdom, tenderness, and greatness in adversity.

It is our effort in this unpretending volume to draw some useful lessons for our guidance in the family, in society, in the church, and in the national government. We have also kept in view the gospel light afforded by these seven chapters, for in the depths of David's heart we see an illustration of the boundless love of God, and in his sorrows he stands as a type of our Lord Jesus Christ.

It was the favour which the original lectures received from those who heard them, that prompted the author to commit them to the press, and the volume is now laid at the feet of Him who sits upon David's throne, for only with His blessing can it be of any service in securing a further allegiance to the King of kings.

W. M. B.

TRENTON, NEW JERSEY.

THE REBEL PRINCE.

CHAPTER I.

Birthplace and Boyhood.

I've learned to judge of men by their own deeds;
I do not make the accident of birth
The standard of their merit.

OUR starting point is one of king David's great unselfish sorrows. Had he been a usurper, or been impatient for the throne which Saul had forfeited, or revengeful toward the hunter after his life, he would have exulted when he heard of the death of the royal persecutor. But no: the fountains of his tenderness were opened, and the great deeps of his heart were broken up. Cæsar wept when he heard that Pompey, his bitterest rival, was dead by other hands than his: with sincerer grief David lamented the fall of the mighty in Israel. Cæsar, after conquering Pompey's sons, was honoured with the title, "Father of his country." David did not seek a victory over Saul's sons, and yet the people were ready to anoint him king over Judah, for he had long been the anointed of the Lord.

9

After he had vented his grief in tears and in song, he "inquired of the Lord, saying, Shall I go up into any of the cities of Judah? And the Lord said unto him, Go up. And David said, Whither shall I go? And he said, Unto Hebron."

That was no mean city. It was associated with ancient and sacred events. No city in Palestine so carries one back to the earliest patriarchal times. It seems to have been the first haunt of civilized men in the land; so ancient that it was built seven years before Zoan in Egypt. Under the oaks of that neighbourhood Abraham had often pitched his tent and raised his altar to the God who had sent him forth to sojourn in the land of promise, as in a strange country, and to join his example with that of our Lord, in teaching us to confess ourselves as strangers and pilgrims on the earth. There, among the olive-groves, had rambled Isaac, the child of promise, before he was chosen for the painful trial of his father's faith. There Sarah, the partner in Abraham's wanderings, and the partaker with him in the promises, had breathed her last, and thence she went to "a better country, that is an heavenly." There was the cave in which was laid the dust of so many of the patriarchs, in the hope of a glorious resurrection. "And from that day to this, it has so come to pass in the providence of God, that no nation or people has had possession of Machpelah, who would have been disposed to disturb the ashes of the illustrious dead within it." And there, doubtless, will rest in peace the dust of Abraham and Sarah, of Isaac and Rebekah, of Jacob and Leah, until God shall bid it rise. It was the only spot that the Father of the faithful ever owned, and no doubt, it will be held for his family until the last day.

Perhaps Joshua and Caleb visited it, when they were honestly spying out the land, and from the neighbouring valley they carried back the goodly Eshcol grapes, as a most acceptable proof of the richness of the promised land. To Caleb, "one of the noblest spirits the nation ever produced," was given Hebron and the vicinity for his possession. It was the old Kirjath-Arba, where dwelt the Anakim, who were so great a terror to the false spies, and of whom they reported, "There we saw the giants, the sons of Anak, which came of the giants, and we were in our sight as grasshoppers, and so we were in their sight." Giants or not, Caleb felt willing to encounter them, and as Moses had promised that "the land whereon his feet had trodden should be his inheritance, and his children's for ever," he asked it, saying, "If so be the Lord will be with me, then I shall be able to drive them out." He drove thence the three sons of Anak, and Hebron became his inheritance, "because that he wholly followed the Lord God of Israel."

Hebron was afterwards appointed as a residence for the Levites, and a city of refuge.* "No place

* "Hebron furnishes another refutation of the ancient fable about

could have recalled more vividly the lessons of departed worth, and the victories of early faith, or abounded more in memorials of the blessedness of following the Lord.   It was a token of God's kindness to David, that he directed him to make Hebron his head-quarters.   And it was a further token of his goodness, that no sooner had David gone up to Hebron, than 'the men of Judah came and anointed him king over the house of Judah.'   It was not all that God had promised, but it was a large instalment."

And now notice David's family.   "David went up thither, and his two wives also, Ahinoam the Jezreelitess, and Abigail, Nabal's wife (widow) the Carmelite† and his men that were with him did David bring up, every man with his household : and they dwelt in the cities of Hebron."   He afterwards won back Michal, his first wife, to prove a source of unabated vexation.   And yet others were added to the number of his wives.   One of these was Maacah, the daughter of Talmai, king of Geshur, whose territory bordered on eastern Manasseh.   His name suggests the three sons of Anak, expelled from Hebron by Caleb, one of whom was

the cities of refuge, *that they were situated in conspicuous positions.* Here it lies in this long valley, with no prospect in any direction except toward the southeast, and even that is not extensive." *Thomson's Land and the Book.*

† Of the Carmel near to Hebron, where Saul was told, "Because thou hast rejected the word of the Lord, he also hath rejected thee from being king." 1 Samuel, xv. xxv.

Talmai. Was the later Talmai a descendant of the Anakim? If so, Absalom had in his veins the blood of the giants, and also retained something of their pugnacious disposition, for he was the son of Maacah. Why David sought the hand of this heathen princess we know not; probably because the alliance seemed of importance to him, in making more permanent the royal power. It was public policy. "He does not appear to have been altogether above the prevalent feeling of the East, which measured the authority and dignity of a court by the rank and connections of the wives of the king." It is painful to record the fact of David's polygamy, but we do not make the fact. We simply state it, without exaggeration or apology.

The six sons of David born in Hebron, were but half-brothers one to another. The son of Maacah was a goodly child, and to him was given a goodly name, full of meaning and of hope. The names given to Hebrew children were often expressive of their future character or career. If this was intended by the parents, it furnishes a clue to their expectations. The name Elisha signified "the salvation of God," and it foreshadowed the mission and character of him who bore it. Gideon was, indeed, "he that bruises or breaks, or he that brings iniquity to an end." To a vigorous child was given the name of Deborah, the Bee. It was prophetic, for such she proved, having "honey for her friends and a sting for her foes." David's

name was fully realized, and not by his parents
alone, for he was truly "beloved" by the nation
and the church of his day, and "dear" to the
heart of the godly through all ages. What prophecy and adaptation in the name given to the babe
of Bethlehem! Jesus, "for he shall save his people from their sins."

Yet many names seem to tell us of the disappointment and the crushed hopes of parents. Eve
called her first-born Cain,—"possession"—as if in
him she already possessed the promised one by
whom the head of the serpent should be bruised.
And yet she lived to see him a murderer. Solomon, probably, indulging the hope that his kingdom would be extended and made more glorious
under the reign of his only royal son, called him
Rehoboam,—one who enlarges, or sets the people
at liberty, or lets the people breathe. But it was
he who said, "I will add to your yoke; my little
finger shall be thicker than my father's loins;
my father chastised you with whips, but I will
chastise you with scorpions." And the people
seeking to breathe, took a wrong course. They
rebelled, and Israel, instead of being enlarged,
was rent for ever. The best of names cannot impart character, nor confer grace.

King David came to know the depths of this
disappointment. He named his oldest son Amnon,
"the faithful and true." A glaring misnomer,
for he proved faithless to all morality, and false to

a sister's love and honour. After being the victim of his baseness she painted him by saying, " Thou shalt be as one of the fools in Israel." David's next son was named Chileab, " the perfection of his father," but either because of early death, or incompetency, the name was never realized in history.

But King David's sorest disappointment was in that brilliant, and most beloved son; the real prince of the blood before Solomon; the only one born of a royal mother. Hoping great things of him, and perhaps intending to make him the heir to the throne, he named him Absalom, " the father's peace," or " the father of peace." He proved anything but either, for he gave his father no peace, and in his manhood, allowed none to the nation while he lived. He was even at war with Jehovah, and perished as the enemy of God.

Of Absalom's boyhood we have no record. The scenery and sacred associations of Hebron could have had but a slight influence upon his character. Before he was seven years of age he was taken away from the city of his birth. The times of his childhood were those of war, when his father took the field and swept many a valley clear of enemies. He may have been old enough to share in the popular excitement caused by the siege of Jerusalem, about eighteen miles distant. He perhaps shouted in delight, when the tidings came that his father had taken the strong hold of Zion, and may

have wished for the day to come, when he might
lead armies to the shock of battle, and smite walled
cities to the dust. It may have been a glad day
for him, when his father removed from Hebron,
and established his family, his court, and his throne
in Jerusalem. Perhaps he stood on the housetop
eagerly watching the splendid procession, march-
ing with shouting and with the sound of a trumpet,
when the ark of the Lord was brought into the
city of David. Perhaps he wished himself one of
the poor boys of the villages, after David had set
the ark in its place, and while he was dealing out
to all the people the choicest cakes and the best of
wine, and when "David returned to bless his
house," perhaps Absalom was one of the first to
greet him, and beg some favour of an indulgent
father.

The services connected with the bringing of the
ark into the city were well adapted to make a most
serious and lasting impression upon the mind of
Absalom, even if he were but a child. Thirty
thousand men of war were present. It was far
more than a grand military parade for the display
of the national strength. It was a glad and solemn
act. Prayers and praises were offered and sung.
A reviving influence must have been felt in all
pious hearts. It was placing in the city the holiest
symbol of God's presence. It was "bringing God
into the capitol," and giving him an habitation.
It was giving him a welcome with the public shouts

of thankfulness, and as the whole multitude sang, "the magnificent volume of sound was, so to speak, the chariot of song, and the horses of song, that bore up this feeling to heaven, and made the service of the church below, a not unworthy echo of the service of the church above." Well does one say of this scene, " I have no notion of hearing, or of any man's ever having seen or heard anything so great, so solemn, so celestial, on this side the gates of heaven."

Yet if it affected Absalom at all, it was not for any lasting good. He from a child rejected God from his own heart. He grieved the Holy Spirit. The soul of King David was exultant with joy, but there were those in his house who had a contempt for revivals of religion. Michal treated his religious fervour with a sarcastic sneer. If Absalom heard her reproach, it must have produced a most hurtful effect. It was freezing every warm emotion that may have been kindled in his soul. Many a child has been injured and hardened in heart by hearing solemn things lightly spoken of, revivals ridiculed, and the earnest manifestations of religious joy treated with the sneers of contempt. Thus perhaps a day of grace passed unimproved by the child Absalom.

2 *

CHAPTER II.

Absalom the Indulged Son.

The faults kings do,
Shine like the fiery beacon on a hill,
For all to see, and seeing, tremble at.

BAD men often furnish good lessons. They reveal to us chapters on the worst side of human nature, so that we may read and be warned. If it be well to look a little into the depths of Satan, it may be even better to gaze down into the astounding depths of human nature, and see what depravities lie there, ready in every man, to break forth with volcanic fury, unless they be extinguished by the Spirit of God. Not Absalom's crimes, rebellion, and death alone, are lessons profitable for us in these our times, but from the home of his youth we may derive hints of errors to be avoided in the rearing of children. From certain facts we may get some insight into his early training.

We can pity King David in his disappointment, and in all the crushing grief that his favourite son caused him to endure. We can pity every parent whose child causes sorrow and shame in a kindly

heart and a godly home. Especially painful is it
to see the sons of some of the most moral and
Christian parents turn out so wretchedly and dis-
gracefully that we almost wonder whether they
ever received at home any reproof, any instruction,
any correction in righteousness. The family tree
may be ancient, and renowned for its goodness,
and yet much of the fruit may be so evil that it
spreads contagion wherever it falls. And the
doctrine is forced upon us that piety cannot be in-
herited by birth. "Grace does not run in the
blood, but depravity does." The worst qualities
of human nature, concealed or suppressed, or almost extinguished in the parents may appear in
their children; but the better qualities, and all the
Christian virtues must come from above. Every
child must be born of God, if there be a sure
escape from the most deadly and disgraceful propen-
sities of our common nature. The best instruction,
alone, cannot purify the youthful heart. Unless
the Dove descend from heaven, and abide upon
the soul, the son of peace and of piety will not
certainly be found in the home of a father who is
as a priest in his house, and a mother who is as an
holy prophetess, teaching and guiding her children.

Why did Absalom prove so unworthy of his
name, so unlike his father, and so fully bent upon
a lawless and rebellious career? Why does any
son of a pious parentage become heedless of holy
precepts, and godly example? Whose fault is it?

The parents are often blamable in this matter. Eli's sons made themselves vile, and he restrained them not. The Bible lays bare this fault in the house of David. If it were possible we would cover it, as did the artist who painted the Macedonian emperor, and hid the scar upon his face. It was an honourable scar, memorable of victory, but still it disfigured the royal countenance. And the painter sketched the monarch, leaning upon his elbow, with his fore-finger covering the scar. So it is with that genuine charity which "covereth a multitude of sins." Instead of exposing the faults of others in scorn and ridicule, it lays over them the finger of love, except when truth and justice require them to be openly rebuked. But charity also "rejoiceth in the truth," and it spares not the faulty when we need to be warned. Inspiration has not hidden this dishonourable scar in the conduct of David. If we could, we would paint him with this flaw screened from view, by the sceptre which he so ably wielded as the best of kings. David's excellencies shine out so brilliantly, that he is like the sun hiding his spots by the dazzling glory of his brightness. It is only by the telescope of the Bible that we detect any dark spots upon the royal character.

Let it not be supposed that we are indulging in the spirit of irreverent criticism, and to guard us let the words of Dr. Kitto be quoted. "Now, the character of David is very dear to us, and he has ever been the object of our sympathy, our admiration, and our love. But truth is dearer to us than even the character of David; and we must not consent to call evil good, and to put darkness for light, because the evil was David's, and the darkness David's. If we were to set about to prove that all David did was right, and the best that could be done, we should not only contradict Scripture, but have work enough upon our hands. Far be it from us to claim for him, that which belongs to One only of all who ever walked the earth. Let us admit the errors and weaknesses of David, as they occur, and our task becomes easy, and his history becomes consistent and clear; but let us uphold him through good and evil, through 'the bitter and the sweet,' and we soon find ourselves ' in wandering mazes lost,' and our perceptions of the broad landmarks between truth and error painfully disordered."

We quote also from another writer,* words . which may apply to many Christians of our own times. "David's slips were like the temporary retiring of the gallant soldier, when fagged and weary, he is driven back for a few moments by superior numbers, but as soon as he has recovered his breath, dashes on undaunted to the conflict. * * With all his slips and falls, there was something in the demeanour of David that showed him to be

* Rev. W. G. Blaikie, in his "David, King of Israel; London,' from which some of the thoughts in this chapter are taken.

cast in another mould from that of other men. He was habitually aiming at a higher standard, and upheld by the consciousness of a higher strength; he was ever and anon directing his view to the secret place of the Most High, taking hold of him as his covenant God, and labouring to draw from him the inspiration and the strength of a nobler life than that of ordinary men."

And once more, as Bengel says, "A swan, plying equally both feet gains upon the water, however turbulent; so David's spirit with all his faults struggled through every difficulty in one general direction. This consoles me about many a disaster, yea, and fault of God's true servants at present."

Have you not been struck by the remarkable fact, that while David was so admirable a governor in the kingdom, he was so unsuccessful a ruler in his own house? He had a splendid management of public affairs. He could plan and execute great enterprises in the state and in the church, in the camp and in the court. He was faithful on the throne as the representative of Jehovah, seeking his counsel, and carrying out his will. In this respect, especially, he was "the man after God's own heart;" the very king who best fulfilled his purposes in the theocracy. But when he came down from that throne into the sphere of home, he did not so ably fill the father's chair. He could hardly have said, "My own dear quiet home, the Eden of my heart," for in this "Paradise of childhood," he

found too much eating of the forbidden fruit, because he gave too much indulgence to his children.

And you ask, why did God permit this? Why
was not this model of a king, also the model of a
father? It is not the royal example that we need,
so much as the paternal example, and why do we
not find it in the father of Absalom? Few kings
will read the pattern set before them, and it seems
to be thrown away; but millions of parents read
of his family government, and why should they not
find everything there for imitation?

Aye, these millions of fathers do have his example, not for imitation, but for warning. Let us
not throw it away. We need both examples. Very
often when the good are speaking to us with gentle voice, and persuasive entreaty, we heed them not.
We do not see the dangers that lie before us. But
when a faulty example roars and thunders its warnings in our ears, we are moved with fear to shun the
errors into which others have fallen. When we know
the very rock upon which a noble ship struck and
shattered the strongest beams, we will not be so
likely to run the risk of wrecking upon it.

And now look at some of the influences in the
home of king David, which must have had their
effect upon Absalom. We learn their existence
and power by inference, but inference is often as
strong as the plainest statement of fact. We are
judging the tree by its fruits; the mode of culti-
vating the field by the harvest which is reaped.

First, there was polygamy—one of the sins, that
even in our goodly land casts its pestilential shadow, and fills a part of it with abominations which
we must not tolerate. The whole force of our laws,
our morality, and our common Christianity ought
now to be set righteously against it, for it is possible that it may be taken up before long by those
who make politics their trade, and a party question
be raised whether our laws shall be executed among
the Mormons? And then it must be very deli-
cately handled in the pulpit, and by the religious
press, or the charge may be brought against us,
that we are preaching politics, and meddling with
party affairs! or we must contend for the right to
declare the whole truth on purely moral questions.
Let us " cry aloud, and spare not," while we have
free opportunity.

Polygamy in David's house may have been a far
less heinous thing than in the home of many a
heathen king. Its evils may have been greatly
modified, yet God's disapproval and punishment
fell upon it. It brought a train of calamities upon
the house, and the heart of the king of Israel, carrying a terrible retribution upon the nation. In
his home there must have been sad confusion, no
unity in principles and plans, in rules and methods,
in teachings and in prayers. He was in every
sense " unequally yoked with unbelievers." And
Absalom must have found enough of rule along
with too much misrule. Instead of the " republic

of home," he doubtless found maternal anarchy of
the wildest sort, and scenes of jealousy and deeply
plotted revenge, that trained him early to be a student of dark envies and grudges, as well as a plot-
ter of conspiracies, and the cool perpetrator of
crafty wickedness. At home, when not under his
father's eye, he may have been schooled in the arts
of intrigue, and in the policies of demagogism and
of rebellion, in which he is an adept when he first
makes his appearance in history. Is it ever true
now, that one parent teaches a child those cunning
arts, by which he may disobey the commands, or
escape the penalties uttered by the other? Do
parents now ever disagree in their methods of
managing their children? Does one make light of
the religion which the other imparts? If so, what
wonder if a son of theirs prove more of an Absalom, than an Isaac, or a Timothy! ·

Secondly, Out of these inharmonious marriages,
with their variances and jealousies, grew other evils,
affecting the father's example. Absalom surely
had the best of precepts from his father, but he
looked also for the best of examples in the life
which was set before him. Every parent who
" gives good precepts, and follows them by a bad
example, is like a foolish man, who should take
great pains to kindle a fire, and when it is kindled
throw cold water upon it to quench it."

Many of David's personal faults and sins arose
from the want of unity, order, and peace in his

3

family, and would not his sons naturally copy them? Many a son imitates his father just far enough to adopt the worst qualities. A parent may have a hundred good traits, and but few bad ones, but the risk of his children imitating the evil traits is far greater than the likelihood of their attaining to the excellencies of his character. Nature inclines to the evil; nothing but the grace of God can incline them to the good, and this grace they may reject. No parent can bestow it. Father or mother may pray for it, and still, as it is a matter of mercy and not of debt, God may rightfully withhold it from a child fully bent upon an evil way.

David was peculiarly rich in the best qualities of nature, and the highest attainment of grace, and hence his few defects only glare the more, and strike boldly on our vision. Absalom and Amnon could easily see them. And these defects are the very ones that appear magnified in his sons. What he did once in "some unguarded hour," became their habitual sins. What he did under strong temptation, they committed of their own accord, out of a passion for the iniquity. What he repented of, and turned away from for ever, they followed after eagerly as hounds hungry for the prey. Where he once fell, but rose again, lifted up by the unseen hand of God and set on the rock, they fell, and went creeping on into the lowest of sins and into perdition. Where he once lusted, they became licentious. Out of a hint from their

father's follies, they formed habits of reckless
wickedness, giving rise to the most dismal tragedies, and leaving their names black with guilt
which time can never wash away. In all their
breathings there was no prayerful psalm rising to
heaven from a penitential heart, "Deliver me from
blood-guiltiness, O God, thou God of my salvation.
Wash me thoroughly from mine iniquity, and
cleanse me from my sin. Create in me a clean
heart, O God, and renew a right spirit within me."

And how does this cry aloud to every parent to
beware of tolerating in ourselves what we would
not have continued and intensified in our children!
The evil that you may have almost overcome, may
appear in your child, and prove its ruin. Let fathers and mothers dwell upon this lesson. Let
them see a father's faults growing into his children's sins, and making his house gloomy with
crime. Let them see his home robbed of its peace
and joy; his sensitive heart pierced through and
through by the shameful conduct of his children;
his oldest son a profligate, and at last slain in a
brother's revenge; his Absalom a traitor and a
daring rebel against his father, his king, and his
God: and how even the "delight he had in Solomon, was only like the satisfaction of a parent
standing on the bleak sea-shore, after a terrible
ship-wreck, with but one child snatched from the
cruel waves," and then they may be safely guarded
against setting an evil example. They will be

careful not to vary one degree from the heavenward point of the compass, lest their children turn
altogether aside unto destruction. "Of all the
gloom which invests the future, no spot seems
darker than that at which a worldly father is
to meet his ruined child—the child whom he himself had professed and vowed to rear for God, and
then led to destruction by walking before the little
one in the broad road to death." Then must the
wail break forth over the lost, "O my son Absalom, my son, my son Absalom! would God I had
died for thee, O Absalom, my son, my son!"

Thirdly, David's best resolutions seem to have
been formed too late to remedy the evils that had
grown up in his house. It was perhaps his painful experience, and the revival of divine grace in
his heart, that led him nobly to resolve upon an
example consistent with his precepts. For he said,
"I will behave myself wisely in a perfect way. I
will walk within my house with a perfect heart.
He that worketh deceit shall not dwell in my
house; he that telleth lies shall not tarry in my
sight." (Psalm ci.)

As he proposes also to "cut off all wicked doers
from the *city of the Lord,*" we may infer that
these resolutions were formed after he was fully
established in Jerusalem. Before they became a
law in his house, Amnon and·Absalom may have
laid the foundations of their characters, and passed
on into the sins of their youth too far to be re-

claimed. His rules seem to have been like *ex post facto* laws—made after the crimes had been committed, and they could not reach back and prevent the errors of his children. The right laws of family government should be adopted before the children know either good or evil, for prevention may secure them against sins, for which there is no human remedy after they have become confirmed habits.

There is another way to learn what were David's later laws of home. Solomon felt and remembered their power over him in his earliest years. "I detect myself to this day," wrote Cecil, "in laying down maxims in my family which I took up at three or four years of age, before I could possibly know the reason of them." They had been parental rules. By this method, as well as by inspiration, Solomon doubtless derived those proverbs for the guidance of children, which cannot fail if rightly applied, for, "Train up a child in the way he should go; and when he is old he will not depart from it." He says, "I was my father's son, tender and only beloved in the sight of my mother. He taught me also, and said unto me, Let thine heart retain my words; keep my commandments, and live."

The career of Solomon was far nobler than that of Absalom. He had a better mother, the excellent Bath-sheba, whom the Rabbins describe as "a woman of vast information and a highly cultivated

3 *

mind, to whose education Solomon owed much of
his wisdom and reputation, and even a great part
of the practical philosophy embodied in the Proverbs." But may we not infer that Solomon had
the benefit of his father's revised code of laws for
the family, which were introduced too late to have
their proper force in restraining and guiding Absalom? Late laws are better than none, for,
though they may not correct the errors of the past,
they may prevent the evils of the future.

Fourthly, It does not seem that David applied
his rules strictly to his older sons. Faults in his
example stand out boldly on the inspired record.
Amnon was deceitful, and still he dwelt in the
royal house. Absalom told lies, and still he tar-
ried in David's sight.

The resolutions of our better moments, when
grace is revived in the heart, are apt to be neglected in seasons when piety is declining, and we
are falling from our steadfastness. Was it thus
with David, a man like us by nature, and as much
in need of daily grace? Was his soul like ours,
yesterday warmed with holy fire, and to-day cold
in worldliness? Had great prosperity an injurious effect upon his fervour of spirit, as we so often find it? Having conquered the nation's foes,
did he cease for a little to make God his shield
against all spiritual enemies? Now, that the
pressure of his former distresses was removed, did
he relax his close walk with God, and allow him-

self to be borne down the stream of his natural in-
clinations? Had he fallen into a luxurious self-in-
dulging mood? We know how it is with ourselves,
and how the family rules adopted in times of revival, when anxious for the salvation of our children, are apt to be neglected when faith grows
feeble and our hearts are cold. Just when our
children most need the kind administration of parental laws, we are likely to be most lax in their
application.

Fifthly, We have evidence of David's over-indul-
gence towards his children, and here the best of
men are most liable to fail. He had an excessive
tenderness of heart, and doubtless of manner. It
is not possible, in one sense, to have feelings too
tender, or a government too kind. But it is possible to allow an excessive gentleness to interfere
with other principles that must have their force in
the successful management of a house. Parents
must sometimes defeat the plans of their children,
disappoint their hopes, deny their requests, check
them in their indulgences, and correct them by
rightful discipline. Some have not the moral courage to do this, and cherish the hope that milder
methods will prevail, and that somehow soft persuasion and tearful entreaty will come at last to
have a meaning, and make a restraining impression.
Eli, and Samuel, and David, seem to have erred
upon this point. They were indulgent. We read
of one of David's children, that, "his father had

never displeased him at any time, saying, Wherefore hast thou done so?"* This was Adonijah, next in age to Absalom. It was he that attempted a new rebellion on the model of Absalom's, but with more crafty management. His father allowed him to run on in his wilful and ambitious way, until the dire effects of parental indulgence came like a sweeping storm upon him in his old age, turning his home into a scene of rivalry and strife, of plots and counterplots, until the heart sickens at such conduct in the house of a man of God.

You may say that David's "failings leaned to virtue's side," and so they did, for tenderness is a grace to be sought from God, but they leaned so hard against paternal virtue, that it was almost pushed over into the dust. Too far east is west, and too great tenderness is cruelty when it ruins a child by indulgence. The Lord does not say of Abraham, I know that he will *entreat* his children, and beg with tears, and plead with wringing hands, and after all indulge them, but he says, "I know that he will *command* them!" He will have order and discipline. "And they shall keep the way of the Lord, to do justice and judgment."

Sixthly, To indulgence was added favouritism. It was David's nature to have some special favourite, for he could not enjoy life without having some

* 1 Kings i. 6.

For further proof of David's readiness to yield to the requests of his children, see 2 Samuel xiii. 6, 7; 23–27; xiv. 32; xv. 7–9.

one on whom to pour the utmost tenderness of his affection. Once it was Jonathan, now Absalom.

It is sometimes urged that a young man is brought up too strictly; there is too much restraining, and hampering, and hedging in; too much catechism and Bible, and urging to church when he does not wish to go. He is tethered at home, and must associate with his father and mother, and keep good hours, and remember the Sabbath-day to keep it holy. He cannot learn the ways of the world, nor study human nature, by mingling with the companions of his choice. Many a sneer is thus cast upon the old Puritanic and Presbyterian modes of family instruction and government.

But under what other system were such men and women ever produced? Such examples of integrity and unwavering principles? Such minds stored with the Bible, that the ploughboy or the weaver could hold a close argument with the doctors of a perverted theology; such hearts of benevolence, blessed of all for the purest outgoings of charity; such spirits strong in the faith that overcomes the world and lays hold on heaven; such heroic souls, that if patriotism required it, they offered themselves in sacrifice for the defence of the land and the liberty they loved; or if truth demanded that one die for it, they were ready for the martyrdom? From what other homes ever went forth such moral giants into this earth of ours? Of whom the world was not worthy, and they left us, and the land grows scarce of them. Until we resort to the same system of godly homes, and establish "God's first church," as it was handed down from Eden, we shall never see their like again. With such homes, there would be "such a church in our land as would make it a praise throughout the whole earth," and such a land that it might well be called Immanuel's.

Under such training there was a strong guard against indulgence and favouritism. But let those who ridicule the strictness of the olden times, and who plead for a method in whose excessive mildness all true government is lost, and religious discipline ignored, have the benefit of an example furnished by the laxer system. There he is, Absalom! Why did not unmingled tenderness win his heart, and special affection secure his obedience? If ever this method had a fair trial, it was then, and the result was, a gifted youth hurrying on to the commission of sin, and driven on to reap its wages in death.

Seventhly, Perhaps David regarded home as a place of rest and enjoyment, rather than a school of instruction, and a church for worship. Men who are burdened with the cares of business, and of office, or daily are worn and weary by labour, are prone to this error.

> From shops and fields, from courts and camps they come,
> To rest their care-worn hearts and weary heads at home.

And well they may. It ought so to be. But

rest is not found in an ungoverned family. Disorder and disobedience must prevent relaxation and enjoyment. The happiest relief from public duties and personal toils, is to find in a cheerful house, obedient children, loving friends, and much of what can make it the earthly type of that future home in the Father's mansions.

Do not urge that court-life, the perplexities of kingship, and the rackings of a royal mind, were an excuse for neglecting the pure example and the godly teachings needed by the sons of David. As well might the exhausting public labours of our Lord have induced him, in his weariness, to refrain from instructing his disciples privately in the things pertaining to the kingdom of God. It was under Oliver Cromwell that England became a might and a glory in the earth. He ruled the nation in the kingly spirit of David, and yet was a model in the government of his family. And on England's throne, to-day, there sits the noblest queen that the world ever saw; remarkable for the moral power she holds over the realm, the purity of her court, and the Christian teaching which she imparts, from her own lips, to her children. And until lately there was a moral power behind that throne—a Prince Albert worthy of universal honour, and a man of enterprise and constant exertion. He instructed and corrected his children as princely father rarely ever did, and in his home he wore that paternal crown better than ever shaded the

brow of a nation's monarch, and second only to
that which he has, doubtless, already received from
his Redeemer's hands. And if ever there be an
Amnon at that court; if ever an Absalom rise up
among the princes of that house, it will not be from
any glaring defects in the royal example, nor from
any deficiency of parental teachings, nor from the
want of any reasons for heartfelt and lasting gratitude.

If king David came from the court, the camp, or
the tabernacle, it was his duty to see that this favourite son was rightly taught and wisely disciplined. Yet that was the very hour when his
bright boy would crave indulgence. It is the dangerous hour when many a father spoils his child.
Yet let us not sit in judgment upon David, the noblest man, and the most thoroughly Christian, portrayed in the Old Testament. Nay, he will judge
us; we have more light than he enjoyed; we have
better opportunities; we are not kings. We have
accumulated warnings; we have Absalom before
us. We have purer examples; our Lord has lived
on the earth. And shall David rise up to condemn
us in the last day? On his dying-bed he could
not but glance back upon his home. "The thought
of disorder there added one pang more to the dying monarch's sorrow, and the complaint uttered
with some of his last breaths was, that his house
was not right with God." Shall this be true of
us? After he has shown us that failures may arise

out of the most tender affection, and that the purest love may be perverted, shall we shiver this ark of a Christian home upon the strand of an inconsistent example, or the fatal rock of parental indulgence?

I have seen a buoy anchored just over a dangerous breaker in the ship's road, rising and rocking by the swell of the tide or the beat of the storm, and in it a bell that struck its mournful warnings as it reeled to and fro, when the morn was misty or the night was dark. And as the captain was running his vessel into port he listened for the stroke of that bell in order to escape the ruin in which others had been involved.

There is a buoy anchored just over this rock of parental indulgence, and the bell, whose every stroke is like a wail over the dead, is loudly ringing its warning in our ears. It is the voice of Absalom the indulged child, who made shipwreck of energies that might have become powerful for good, and of a soul freighted with some of the highest natural endowments.

4

CHAPTER III.

The Sinner's Victory.

We are not worst at once. The course of evil
Begins so slowly, and from such small source,
An infant's hand might stem the breach with clay;
But let the stream get deeper, and philosophy,
Age, and religion, too, shall strive in vain
To turn the headlong torrent.

ADMITTING the force of David's errors in family
government, we must remember that Absalom was
not compelled to give them the controlling influence in the formation of his character. Why did
he not avoid that which his own conscience condemned, and follow that which his best judgment
approved? He must have known that his father's
faults were greatly overbalanced by his excellencies. Was he excused,—is any young man now
excused, by saying, "There are faults in my father's conduct and character"? Surely not, for a
personal responsibility rests upon every son, whatever be the errors of a parent.

Even suppose that David had been destitute of
those godly virtues which so vastly preponderate in
his character, and had been positively wicked, this

would not be an apology for Absalom in throwing off the better influences that surrounded him, and in steeling his heart against the power of the truth, of conscience, and of the Spirit of God. Who lays all the blame upon the godless Rehoboam, in accounting for the fact that his son Abijam " walked in all the sins of his father which he had done before him" ? Upon Abijam must rest the greater blame for the course he took. The son of a wicked man is responsible for being like his father.

From the homes of godless men have sometimes come forth sons who have feared, loved and served the Lord. Ahaz was the most unlike David, and the most corrupt king that had sat upon Judah's throne, respecting neither the Lord, the law, nor the prophets. Yet his son Hezekiah avoided the sins of his father, and became eminent as a king and as a saint. So with Asa. Josiah too had an impious and idolatrous father, but shunning the royal example, he accepted God as the guide of his youth; and this young king was in Judah what Edward the Sixth was in England, the marvel of history. Why did not Absalom form such a character, and qualify himself to do that which was right in the sight of the Lord?

The case is much stronger against Absalom, when we take into account his father's eminent piety and devotion to the church of God. The son of every Christian father is greatly responsible for the course he takes in life. Who charges npon

John Howard all the blame for the reckless course taken by his only son? That son first allowed himself to become "a prey to those who combine artfulness with vice;" then he let a contempt for his father creep into his heart; then he formed vicious habits, and at last he ran swiftly into mental and moral ruin.

Who was ever heard to apologize for Absalom? Even Judas, the thief and the traitor, has found an apologist, in our day, who attempts to palliate his conduct in betraying our Lord for thirty pieces of silver. But no one raises a mild plea for this first great rebel in Israel.

We have no sight of him during the younger years when he was forming his habits, and determining his character. We do not see him growing worse and worse by slow degrees. We do not see evil associations gradually gathering around him, and gaining upon him by insinuation, by allurement, by bolder temptations, and by boon companionships. But when he first appears in history, he stands before us complete in character, accomplished in artifices, cool and hardy in revenges, daring in his policies, and desperate in hazarding liberty and life. And why? How has he come to such a high pitch of heartless wickedness? How have his features become so fixed that he can go unblushing into crime, and his nerves so like "strings of steel" that he can deliberately plan and execute a murder? Ah! he has had a victory

—one that hundreds are, to-day, struggling to gain. It is *the sinner's victory!*

Such coolness and self-complacency, such readiness for iniquity and boldness in it, such bravery against the fear of justice, and such deliberate violation of the law of God, were not born in Absalom, nor in any one now who has reached the point where history and justice began with him. They were acquired. They cost many a struggle, and much fighting against conscience, truth, and God. Depraved as we all are by birth, no one in his first years is so desperate that he can commit the crimes of Absalom with his self-possession and hardihood. That face blushed in infancy, which now is bronzed in manhood. He once was sensitive, who now is "past feeling." There is a class of sins peculiar to children, less heinous than those which are peculiar to men. There may be "precocious depravity," but in the sinner, generally, it is something that "grows with his growth, and strengthens with his strength." There is an onward march in sin as well as in grace. There is a victory for the sinner over the good, the true, and the holy, as well as a triumph for the Christian over the evil, the false, and the tempting. What then does every young man do, who attains to a character such as we find in Absalom when he entered upon the career which the God of inspiration has deemed it wise to portray for our instruction? What is the sinner's victory?

4 *

First. He conquers much in himself. Not the evil, not the predisposition to be a wanderer from the path of duty and of life, not the natural indifference to religion, nor the depravities that cannot be expelled except by the Holy Spirit, but he overcomes the better tendencies which God has given to restrain and direct him. Once he felt the power of conscience, of fear, and of love. They caused his blood to bound through all his being when he thought of committing a known sin. His heart beat in fear, conscience burned in his breast, his mind was restless, and his cheek flushed as he sought for courage to perform an evil deed. Convictions often ran, like lightning, through his soul. He started from his dreamy sleep as if he heard the voice of God. And when putting forth his hand to sin, he glanced with restless eye on every side to see if any human witness was looking on, and he had to fight that piercing thought, "Thou, God, seest me!" It was a struggle against all his better convictions, and against everything that represented God in his soul. And after occasional sins became habits, he tried not to feel any convictions of conscience, but still the arrows of the Almighty went shivering through his soul. Thus the battle went on, until at length the baser passions of his nature rose to help him in the struggle. They stifled conscience. They put down his self-respect. They drowned the memories of truth. They drove out the fear of God.

And now he can sin boldly, coolly, deliberately. He has hardened himself to iniquity. If conscience reprove, he knows how to sear it until it shall trouble him no more. If fears arise, he can lull them to sleep. If shame burn in his heart, he can quench its fire. This is one victory.

Secondly. He overcomes the influences of the truth, and the effect of church ordinances. The law of God must often have been read in the ears of Absalom. The young Hebrew could scarcely have passed a day without hearing the word of the Lord from parent, prophet, or priest. The tabernacle invited him to come to the altars of God, not only with a lamb, but with the sacrifices of a broken heart and a contrite spirit. The cloud of incense invited him to prayer, and voices of song to praise. If he needed instruction or advice, there was the good Nathan, who seems to have been the prophet of the court, and tutor of the king's sons. How could he go on unaffected by all these privileges, unless he made an effort to resist them?

Many a one now hardens himself to resist the appeals and persuasions that fell from the lips of the Son of God, and that still are urged by the ministers of truth. He triumphs over them. He castles himself in cold indifference, and fortifies his soul with excuses, or doubts, or delusions. He bars the door against the entrance to that word which giveth light. He sets his shield against the arrow drawn from the gospel quiver, and smiles to

see it fall shattered at his feet. He boasts that
preaching which arouses others does not affect him.
Men wonder at his coolness, but he admires their
astonishment. No exhortation disturbs his com-
posure, no entreaty softens his heart. Not even
does the word judgment, or eternity, stir a ripple
on the smooth surface of his thoughts. This is
another victory, gained by the power of his resistance.

Thirdly. He conquers the influence of parents,
friends, and godly associates. Their kindness is
abused. The tenderness of David toward Absalom would have had a good effect, had not the son,
in his perversity, taken advantage of it. He despised the riches of such human goodness, forbearance and long-suffering. He overcame the force
of love, entreaty and persuasions. When a young
man can do this, he is not far from ruin. "He
that hateth reproof shall die." When too late, he
may exclaim in his remorse, " How have I hated
instruction, and my heart despised reproof, and
have not obeyed the voice of my teachers, nor inclined mine ear to them that instructed me!"

In the dens of many an infamous lane, in many
a pestilential cellar, in many a prison's gloomy
cell, on the deck of many a pirate ship, in many a
robber's cave or counterfeiter's garret, and on
many a strange shore whither the guilty have fled
from a justice whose eye was on the watch and
whose feet were shod for swift pursuit, may be

found one who once had a kind and Christian home but rebelled against its peaceful government, and casting away the Bible, and trying to expunge every memory of godly counsels and tearful prayers, ran to an excess of riot, bringing a father's gray hairs in sorrow to the grave, and driving a mother to a refuge in God's mercy, that she might find some relief from the anguish caused by an ungrateful, wandering child.

Fourthly. He overcomes the impressions made upon his soul by the providences of God. Once every unusual mercy or event affected him, but now the blessings of Heaven come and go, and he scarcely recognizes them. The goodness of God does not lead him to repentance. Judgments may be abroad, but he does not learn righteousness. Sickness does not enforce upon him the solemnities of death, judgment, and eternity. Losses on earth do not cause him to seek after treasures in heaven. A death is not heard saying to him, "prepare to meet thy God." These impressions he has overcome. They pass unheeded by, and he remains the same.

Fifthly. He succeeds in resisting the Spirit of God. Often has the heavenly Dove descended upon him, but he has grieved him away. Often has the Spirit's flame been kindled, but he has quenched it. Perhaps the Holy Spirit no longer strives with him, and he is left to follow the way that he has chosen.

This may appear very bold and brave. It may seem to be the mighty strength of a successful opposition. It may seem the achievement of independence and liberty. But it is really the most daring of all rebellions. Absalom's first great rebellion was against God.

It is a fearful thing to reach that point in character when truth, holy ordinances, Christian friendships, and the Holy Ghost seem to make no impression upon the soul. So long as these had any power over Absalom, he could not be the young man that we find him when he first appears in history. We do not say that he took just the steps we have described, but we do say that any young man who takes them, will reach his point in hardness of heart.

How often a newspaper brings before us the name of a young man heretofore unknown to the world, but all at once made notorious! Yet you know that the first crime that goes upon the public record is not really the first in his life, nor the only one written in the book of God. You know that he has long been preparing for it; seasoning, hardening, and growing toward it. For conscience, reason, self-respect, honour to parents, regard for society, fear of law, reverence for the Bible and for God, were enough to have held him in restraint. Any one of them was enough to check him, and surely all of them combined were sufficient to have strengthened him against the temptations to crime.

And they would have so proved, had he not overcome their power. It was his victory.

Fearful triumph! For he has not conquered sin.
Nay, it has dominion over him. He may be given
over to reap for ever what he has sown. He may
overcome the means and agencies of grace, but he
cannot conquer Jehovah! He must come at last
to a point where he cannot succeed, and that point
is the Divine Justice. Before it he must break
down, and let it rule over him for ever. "It is a
fearful thing to fall into the hands of the living
God!" May he save us from Absalom's first great
error and rebellion!

Far be it from us to say that Absalom had fully
attained to such hardness of heart, that he was left
entirely to himself, and that it was too late for him
to repent. Nor would we declare of any one living that the Spirit of God had taken from his soul
his everlasting flight. Some who long indulged
their evil natures, long resisted holy influences, and
seemed to have overcome conscience, truth, love,
and persuasion, have at length ceased fighting
against God, and have permitted King Jesus to
rule over them. We know the story of the prodigal son. We remember Augustine and Newton.
We are told of one who went so far that "the
standard of home was no longer in his mind; he
defied the restraints of a widowed mother, and fled
from her vicinity that he might not be hampered
by her urgency or example. For two years he led

a guilty wanderer's life. But on one occasion, during his Sabbath orgies, he was invited by an aged believer to enter a house of God which he was passing, in company with one as lawless as himself. The suggestion awoke for a moment the recollection of former days. He complied, and the sight of parents with their children worshipping their God, did for him what hunger did for the prodigal son. The past affected the present, and the wayward youth was reclaimed." He passed through a severe struggle, but gained the victory. At length he went to Africa as a missionary, where he tried to win souls as he had once tried to ruin his own.

Is anything too hard for God? Will not Christ save even unto the uttermost, them that call upon him? Let every one answer such questions on the side of hope and mercy, yet may we all remember at what a fearful risk one may resist the truth and the Holy Ghost. There may still be those of whom God declares, " For that they hated knowledge, and did not choose the fear of the Lord; they would none of my counsel; they despised all my reproof; therefore shall they eat of the fruit of their own way and be filled with their own devices."

There is another victory—one for him who in God's name and help, conquers the evil in himself, and the temptations around him, putting sin, and death, and hell under his feet. He triumphs by faith, obedience, love and prayer; and his life-thought and death-song will be in all conflicts and sufferings, "In all these things we are conquerors, yea, more than conquerors through him that loved us!"

A single sentence was once heard falling from the lips of an earnest man. It was, "O Lord, give me another victory!" He had certainly gained one triumph. Was it over passion? Over an evil thought? Over the temptations of avarice? Over resentment? Over the tendency to neglect an important duty? Over an old habit? We know not. But he had evidently wrestled against more than flesh and blood, and triumphed by the power of God's grace and Spirit. From the battle-field of his own soul he had come off the victor. Alexander was never so happy, for Alexander never conquered himself.

And now some other attack was feared. He saw the conflict before him, and the strength of his foe. Could he resist it? Could he drive the enemy from the field? Must he be overcome of evil? Could he overcome evil with good? There was danger, and looking above for help, he prayed, "O Lord, give me another victory!"

These victories! They are the means of growth, strength, assurance and rejoicing. Gain one, and the next is more easy. Not an hour will pass but we shall have some besetting sin haunting us, some old habit on our track, some splendid cheat of the

5

tempter alluring us, some forbidden thought, emotion, or purpose plotting to betray us, and some
innate depravity warring against us; and then we
shall need to pray for *another victory.*

These triumphs! They are not heralded in the
papers, nor do men hasten to the "News-offices"
to learn the result of the last struggle for a soul.
They are written in the Book of Life. They are
published in heaven, and angels rejoice over one
sinner who has gained a triumph over the destroyer.
"Thanks be unto God, who giveth us the victory
through our Lord Jesus Christ!"

CHAPTER IV.

Absalom the Lawless Avenger.

Even nature will exceed herself, to tell
A crime so thwarting nature.

MANY of the worst and oftenest committed sins
are those which must be pointed out only by the
most delicate reference; hinted, rather than
broadly named. It is not always a mere fastidious
taste that requires this, but a high moral sense of
propriety.

And yet the delicate portrayal may be the more
dangerous method, for vice may be clothed in at-
tractive beauty. Lord Byron drew so fair a picture of licentiousness that it charms rather than
warns his more susceptible admirers. Shakspeare
had a way of bluntly saying just what he meant,
and he makes this vice appear shameful, disgust-
ing, detestable, and utterly execrable. You are
not offended with him, but you want the odious
sin driven from the earth. It is well that the Bible is a plain book, and gives every sin its right
name, or some vices might not receive their proper
treatment in dainty times.

The first chapter of Absalom's career is recorded as with the point of a diamond, guided by the most delicate hand. It is hard to make a bad thing look well, even in the wisest words. The abominable deed of Amnon is described as tenderly as the gross subject would permit. If any suppose it not fit to be publicly read, surely it is unfit to be privately imitated.

Yet inspired wisdom has given us this chapter in the bold and fearless march of truth. What merely human writer would have placed it in a book to be the moral guide in all nations and ages? Any mere moralist would have shrunk from the tempest of scorn and reviling which such a page would draw upon it; or trembled lest the evil effects of the story would overbalance the good. "None but God could have the fearless fortitude to place in the Holy Bible this narrative of sin and shame." He knew it would be needed even where civilization holds her sway, lest society should imagine that vices are cured when they are only concealed, and men should still commit "the oldest sins in newest kind of ways."

It may surprise us that this nameless sin, against which God saw best to publish the seventh commandment, is not yet driven out of civilized society, and far across the borders of Christendom. It may surprise us, that, with all this delicate taste there is not true refinement enough to make it so rare in every community, that none need longer to

cry aloud and spare not. It stands as one of the
most frequent on the records of crime. It is one
of the most common of those which are published
every week. It withers and blasts a large amount
of the strength of our land. It stalks abroad in
the open day; shows its shameless front on our
streets; sets its decoys and encouragements in
almost every secular newspaper; bids for new vic-
tims in most of our "dailies"—flings even a bolder,
profaner literature before thousands of our youth,
and presents the most formidable temptations
which they have to encounter. Nor does it lurk
alone in the lower ranks of society; it steals in
upon high life, and high position, creeping into
marble halls and stately palaces. It fastens upon
the gifted and the gay, the accomplished and the
honourable, and makes an utter waste of their being. It is to-day running riot over health and
happiness, over law and life. It is dogging the
soldier with the tiger's stealthy tread, and whispering in the ear of the unsuspecting student. It
is scattering its poison everywhere, until poverty
and prisons help to declare the extent of its power.

Yet it cries out that it must be let alone, because
it is offensive to lift aloud the warning voice! Our
Lord declared against it in the plainest terms, and
we cannot be charged with going beyond the
bounds of prudence if we follow his example, and
that of his apostles. We must speak, while it
rages, for it hardens the heart, more than almost

any other sin, against the very gospel which is
proclaimed to reform, regenerate, and restore the
guilty to the favour of God. There can be no
prevalent morality where it is tolerated; no social
virtues where it is not branded with infamy.

It may surprise us that in the commission of
any sin there can be so much coolness and deliberation. There may be some extenuation if the act
be impulsive, and the temptation come suddenly
with almost resistless power. But too often a
crime has no such apology. It has been thought
of, and deliberately planned. Imagination has
dwelt upon it. Even the counsel of some base
Jonadab has been gladly received. It has been
talked about with a third party in the plot. Far
gone must he be, who can tolerate an accessary in
a crime abhorrent to all decency and self-respect!
Amnon's crime was not simply an unguarded act;
it was one of the coolest ever committed. None
but an adept in the arts of vice, who had by slow
degrees reached this extravagant pitch of heart-
lessness, could have so deliberately carried out his
villainous designs.

You abhor, then, this victimizer while you pity
the unsuspecting victim, and you are not astonished
at the record, that "when King David heard of all
these things he was very wroth." He had reason
to be. It was a burning disgrace. It was a stain
upon the family. It would excite the tongue of
slander. It would be whispered in the city, and

raise a noise at the court. No sin more readily
arouses a disposition to avenge the injured and
punish the guilty. No crime causes a parent or
brother to feel more keenly what justice is, and
how deserved is a righteous severity. You expect
then that the king will bring from the Jewish law
the terrible penalty of death, fixed by Jehovah,
and then with Roman courage visit it upon the
guilty though he be the eldest son, and the heir to
the throne. For when men of mildness and extreme tenderness are once provoked by justice,
they punish with unflinching rigor. With them
anger is the "resentful spark that flies from the
struck shield," and him on whom it falls it burns
with punishment.

But no! David was "very wroth"—that was
all. He did nothing. He must have grieved unspeakably. He must have wished that he had
more carefully disciplined his son; wished that the
awful thing had never happened: wished that it
could be undone; wished almost everything indeed,
but yet he did nothing. Was he quite stupefied
at finding that the evils pronounced by the prophet
as a retribution upon himself, were falling thicker
and heavier upon his family? Was he so stunned
that he could not lift his hand to punish? Or was
he so exceeding tender that he hoped milder measures would secure a better result? Was he blind
to the fact that if this sin were not punished, another more desperate would follow? And if sins

went on redoubling, calamities would also be re-doubled, for if justice were left for God, it would be measured out in full upon crime? Let the mantle of charity cover the king, while his heart is wrung with anguish and his eye is raining tears.

Amnon goes on unarrested, unpunished. Perhaps he is not disgraced at court, nor refused the social attentions, (for we have seen it thus!) while Tamar remains desolate in her brother Absalom's house. We hear of her no more, unless in regard for her, Absalom calls a daughter by her name.

> At her the lip of Scorn may curl,
> At her Society may hurl
> Society's disdain.

But there is one human eye fixed upon this guilty man; there is one young prince who is determined that this outrage shall be avenged. And he is Absalom. At first sight we are almost ready to give him credit for a high sense of honour, and for a just indignation. For when he is the only one to whom an injured sister can look for protection, he offers her his guardianship, counsel, and home. Also the contempt which he showed towards his guilty half-brother, would seem almost honourable if he had aimed his hatred at the sin rather than at the sinner. "He hated Amnon." We do not wonder. He ought to have hated the crime, even while pretending to recognize the criminal as his brother. But this was too nice and moral a distinction for him to perceive.

If it were the sin that he desired punished, why
not take up the law and bring the guilty to a legal
trial? Was the law against this great iniquity a
dead letter? Then what glory for him to bring it
forth from its grave and restore it to life and
power! What a chance to prove himself a refor-
mer of crime, a restorer of law, an upholder of justice, an advocate of the wronged, and a terror to
evil-doers! What a judge he might have been, as
he afterwards wished to be! The path was open,
but he slighted this opportunity of entering upon a
noble career.

But he was not frowning with intolerance upon
the sin; he hated Amnon. It was not, therefore,
legal justice that he sought, but private revenge.
Silently he brooded over the wrong, and under the
guise of honour he plotted a brother's death.
From the hour of the outrage he determined that
Amnon should die. If the mode of settling such
affairs by the duel had been known among the He-
brews we might expect to find it here, for Absalom
was the very man, and this the very time, for him
to have sent the offender a challenge. Arguments
have been urged for this murderous way of settling
disputes. A system of rules has been laid down
for conducting it. It has even been called by the
dignified title of the "code of honour"! Under
this pretentious name it has prevailed in our land.
But its apologists could never cite a case from the
Bible, and wrest it as many have done the Scrip-

tures to support a great sin. No longer let it be
regarded as chivalrous, but barbarous, inhuman,
murderous.

Was it revenge alone that was prompting Absalom in all his quiet plans? There seems to be a
deeper motive for this hushed wrath, this pretended
sense of honour, this cautious policy. There seems
to be something else nurturing in this cunning mind
and crafty heart.

The throne—that seems the object of his ambition. Dr. Kitto says, "He intended to make his
revenge effectual, and to use it for clearing his way
to the throne. We cannot but think that he had
already taken up the design upon the kingdom
which he eventually carried out, and that, as Amnon was his elder brother and the heir-apparent,
he meant to use his private wrong as the excuse
for removing so serious an obstacle from his path.
But to this end it was necessary that the king, as
well as Amnon, should be lulled into the conviction
that he had no thoughts of revenge, and that the
matter had gone from his mind."

And now see the wary, wily politician of the unscrupulous school; the man who makes any means
foul or fair aid him in reaching his ambitious ends;
the man who watches and waits for the favourable
moment when he may strike the decisive blow, and
remove the barrier to his hopes. Ambition is
wrong when it aims at a wrong object, and goes
upon the principle of making the end justify the

means. It is then a cruel passion, clutching at what other persons possess, crowding them from the places they deserve to hold, trampling upon their rights, and sometimes making crime the way to power. It has strong temptations for every young man among us, and he must be well fortified by religious principles who can resist it. Dr. Payson, after reading certain biographies, wrote thus to a young man: "Two of these characters agreed in saying that they were never happy until they ceased striving to be great men. The remark struck me, as you know the most simple remark will, when God pleases. It occurred to me at once, that most of my sorrows and sufferings were occasioned by my unwillingness to be the nothing that I am, and by a constant striving to be something. I saw that if I would but cease struggling, and be content to be anything or nothing, as God pleases, I might be happy." Here religious principles had not been laid aside. What then of that ambition in which they are ignored, and,

> Faith, honor, justice, gratitude and friendship
> Discharged at once?

Absalom must first take time: Rashness and sudden impulse might defeat his plans. He must appear quite indifferent to the outrage committed. And he takes time. Two full years pass away. He speaks not a word to Amnon, good or bad, lest they may wrangle and bring on the crisis at the wrong hour. Policy can keep his anger from boil-

ing over, and defeating a calmly-plotted scheme.
And on that silent wrath the sun goes down every
day for two years. If there be such danger, as
the Apostle Paul intimated, in letting the sun go
down one day upon a man's wrath,—for thus he is
giving place to the devil—then what would more
than seven hundred sunsets do? Absalom must
be giving a large place in his heart to the devil,
and becoming full of his wiles. He can plan a
successful tragedy.

Next he must lull all suspicion. Not a whisper
was breathed of his intentions. Probably not a
man walked the streets of Jerusalem with a fairer
speech than Absalom. Mercy for Amnon was on
his lips, while murder was in his heart. No one
suspects that when the fraternal "looks are sweet
as summer, they will soon fall blighting and blast-
ing as the winter frosts."

Next he must find an occasion. He lays part
of his plot in the country. Eight miles out he has
an estate, and preparations are making for a great
sheep-shearing festival. He now changes his policy, and all at once becomes very gracious and
given to hospitality. He will play the friend, the
forgiving brother, the affectionate son. He invites
the king and all his sons, and urges their attend-
ance. But David declines, for he prudently counts
the cost, and wishes to save the prince the ruinous
expense of a royal visit. It is a delicate hint upon
economy.

"Then let my brother Amnon go with us." The feast will be dull enough unless the heir-apparent be there! King David does not suspect that the festival will be a funeral if he be there, and yet he has some misgivings. "Why should he go with thee?" Do you not remember? Are you not afraid to trust him? Can you trust yourself when feasting with one that you have hated? But the smooth earnest words of Absalom lull the fears of the king, and gain the one thing without which all the plot must fail. Amnon goes to the festival like a fatted ox unconscious of the slaughter, and Absalom goes with his father's blessing upon him. Like this, perhaps, the benediction ran.

> "The Lord bless thee and keep thee:
> The Lord make his face to shine upon thee,
> And be gracious unto thee;
> The Lord lift up his countenance upon thee,
> And give thee peace."

Under the weight of a father's blessing Absalom hastes to the tragedy that he had planned. It reminds us of the assassins—Gerard who stealthily murdered William the Silent, for example—who were shrived by a priest, and with his blessing upon them, walked boldly to plunge the dagger into the heart of the innocent. O Absalom! if thy father's hand and voice have been lifted upon thee, how darest thou fulfil thy plot!

Great was the feast, and the mirth ran high. Smiling servants were ready to strike or stab, and

G

when " Amnon's heart was merry with wine," Absalom gave the word, ordering his men to be " courageous and valiant," and the guilty prince, who had gone two years safe from punishment for his heartless crime, was despatched by a brother who had deeply laid his plot, set the trap, sprung it upon his victim, and made himself a murderer !

It was an aggravation of this second great crime in David's family, that it was not only done by a brother, done in cold blood, and through treachery, but at the moment when Amnon was " least apprehensive, least able to resist, and least fit to go out of the world." As if the avenger's malice aimed to destroy both soul and body, without giving his victim opportunity to call for mercy from God with his last breath. Death, long devised and unsuspected, fell upon him when he was overcharged with mirth and drunkenness. Thus the lawless criminal fell by lawless revenge.

Here is a sin, with which the moral taste is not offended by the plainest speech. No delicacy is needed here. Horrible as it is, it can be named—murder. We are not likely to come in danger of this atrocious crime, but there are certain things very common among us, that have a murderous tendency. Hatred runs so strongly in this direction that it is declared by Him who knows the human heart, " He that hateth his brother is a murderer."

There is a difference between sin and crime. Sin

dwells in us, as a disposition to do evil.   Crime is
an act.   Sin may lie in the nature, slumbering or
suppressed.   Crime is the outward development of
the hidden depravity.   God not only regards the
criminal act, but the indwelling sin that leads to it.
Both of the lawless crimes, so fearfully pictured in
this chapter, proceed from the heart.   In the progress towards the first, there are various degrees
of criminality.   There are impure thoughts, imaginations, and suggestions.   There are wicked covet-
ings and the courting of temptation.   And then
the launching forth upon the dark tempestuous sea
of piratical licentiousness.   Few venture, without
hurrying on to complete destruction.   Few ever
return from the presumptuous voyage.   Erect all
the light-houses you will upon safe shores, and
make broad the harbours, yet very few will turn
thither for salvation.   How this dark sin declares
to us in solemn warning, " Keep thy heart with all
diligence."

And this heart-depravity may develop toward
murder.   In its indulgence of envy, hatred and revenge it is really wishing to take away another's
happiness, and it may, possibly, go on in the same
direction until it may take away another's life.
The heart first slays, and then the hand finishes
the victim.   This, also, loudly proclaims, " Keep
thy heart with all diligence, for out of it are the
issues of life."

Every one who has a living conscience, and a

love for social peace and safety, has a strong desire to see crime justly punished. A whole community, often, rises up and demands it. Yet the executors of justice may, sometimes, be too slow, or may blink at iniquity. The Amnons and the Absaloms may be permitted to go unarrested and unpunished. In such a case certain men take up the cause of the injured, on their own responsibility, and let a just resentment against the injurer grow into a dark revenge. This is a passion carrying many a noble nature astray, and perpetually involving the human race in troubles. It is everywhere, inspiring a large share of the injuries inflicted by one man upon another. Every lawyer can tell you that a great proportion of his clients are not seeking justice, but revenge.

Generous souls may be infected with it. Robert the Bruce was generous, yet extremely passionate, and in his rashness was unrelenting and cruel. With all his nobleness, he did not refrain from plunging the dagger into the heart of the treacherous Comyn, even in the convent of the friars. And well does the historian note, that this rash revengeful deed was followed by the marked displeasure of Heaven, for no man ever went through more misfortunes when all the providences seemed arrayed against him, although he rose at last to exalted position and honor.

Revenge seems to be the favourite passion with dramatists, for it so naturally works up its own

fearful tragedy that the writer may but record actual realities, without inventing characters or deeds.
It works up many an unwritten tragedy in social
life. And is it not a sad proof of human depravity,
that tragedies afford such natural pictures of human nature? Why must we say that they are so
natural, so true to life? Only because we see
constantly so much of revenge and its terrible
workings, that the worst deeds appear most life-
like. Indeed it makes all history dramatic. What
is past history but the plotting, the betraying, the
avenging, and the murdering, which have kindled
their quenchless fires through all ages? Occasion-
ally a heroic nature, a generous spirit, a magnani-
mous character appear, but if revenge did not
sometimes prompt them to ignoble deeds, they were
at least forced to stand like a ·rock against its
shafts, so that they shattered where they struck.

Let us not forget that the field is one on which
we are often brought, and on which some of our
best victories may be won. Seldom a day passes
without an occasion for practising the advice, "Say
not, I will do so to him as he hath done to me."
One of the effects of a regenerating Christianity is
the casting out of this evil spirit, and the introduc-
tion of patience under injustice, and the forgiveness of injuries. The battle fought on this field
may not be attended with the honours of ordinary
contests; there are no medals, no stars of reward;
but they are registered in heaven, and to such vic-

6 *

tories, in part, is the promise made by the Captain of our salvation, " To him that overcometh, will I grant to sit with me on my throne, even as I also overcame and am set down with my Father on his throne."

Yes, Jesus overcame. No malevolence dwelt in him; no malice, no hatred, no disposition to revile when he was reviled, nor to call down fire from heaven upon those who shut their gates against him, nor to pray for vengeance upon those who crucified him, and mocked him upon the cross. " Let this mind be in you which was also in Christ Jesus."

These dark pictures so visible in the beginning of Absalom's career, cause us to turn to one drawn by a Saviour's hand, showing us, not only how to be guarded against every tendency to these enormous crimes, but to be regenerated from the depravities in which they originate, and sanctified from indwelling sin until the soul is made whiter than snow. " Blessed are the pure in heart, for they shall see God."

They are not unwilling to have God see them. Beneath his eye they are full of light. The shining in of the Sun of righteousness drives away the darkness and the pestilential vapour that have lain upon the soul. Every passion, that, like a wild beast of the night, has been ravening for its prey, is banished, and the heart is made to bloom like Eden, and flourish as the garden of the Lord. The

thoughts are directed toward God; the memory
lingers on his loving-kindness, the imaginations are
upward toward heaven, and the growing wish of
the soul is for that vision of beauty when we shall
see Jesus as he is, and be like him. Every man
that hath this hope in himself, purifieth himself,
even as he is pure.

And while the blessed are seen by the eye of
God, they are not afraid to look upon him. They
see him in the pure heart where God is more than
mirrored—he is imaged there. Let science photo-
graph the sun; this is not the greatest wonder.
The transcendent miracle is that the soul, prepared
by the Holy Ghost, may receive the very image of
God. In the soul there may be godliness—God-
likeness. No dead picture is it; it lives, it breathes.
It is the soul created anew in Christ Jesus. We
live, we breathe, we see, as never before. We see
God by the indwelling power of holiness, and we
shall see yet him, by the pure spirit's sight, in
heaven.

> Finish, Lord, thy new creation;
>   Pure and spotless may we be;
> Let us see thy great salvation
>   Perfectly restored in thee:
> Changed from glory into glory,
>   Till in heaven we take our place;
> Till we cast our crowns before thee,
>   Lost in wonder, love, and praise.

CHAPTER V.

Absalom the Fugitive.

Now conscience wakes the bitter memory,
Of what he was, what is, and what must be
Worse.

ABSALOM has outgeneraled himself. He has
struck a deadly blow that may speedily recoil upon
him, and has raised an uproar too great for him to
endure. The rumour flies to the court, growing as
evil tidings ever grow upon their way, and making
bad even worse, until the report is, "Absalom hath
slain all the king's sons, and not one of them is
left." David is overwhelmed.

Soon the truth follows, and yet it is hard to allay the king's fears, and convince him that his
other sons are yet alive. Does he suspect that
Absalom was capable of so extended a slaughter?
Jonadab, the cousin of Amnon, and partaker in his
sin, is subtil enough to curry favour with the king
by endeavouring to soothe his mind. "Let not
my lord the king take the thing to his heart, to
think that all the king's sons are dead; for only
Amnon is dead." David can scarcely credit this

informer, who has a personal motive in being officious, and who must labour to make himself believed, by telling the same thing over and over.
The watchman sees a crowd of people panic-stricken
and bewildered, hasting down the hill, and Jonadab
exclaims, "Behold, the king's sons come! As thy
servant said so it is." They reach the place where
they and the king and the people weep together in
great excitement, confusion, and grief.

David, so overcome by his feelings, and by the
bewilderment of the people, quite overlooks the
baseness of Jonadab, when he declares that Absalom had determined this slaughter from the very
hour that he felt his honour touched. This officious hanger-on about the court betrays himself.
He has known the plot—has kept it from Amnon
whom he once helped into sin—has not informed
the king, and has not interfered with Absalom in
the work of private revenge. It is well if this low
mean actor in the tragedy has not been as guilty
of Amnon's death as he was of his treacherous sin.
He might have prevented both, but now may be
suspected as an accomplice, by his own words.
David was peculiarly sensitive to everything like
baseness, and we almost wonder that he does not
serve this news-bearer as he did the Amalekite who
brought him the crown and bracelet of Saul with
the lying boast that he had slain him, exclaiming,
"Thy blood be upon thy head; for thy mouth hath
testified against thee."

If David, in his astonishment and grief, over-looks such baseness, we are not surprised that no order is given for Absalom's arrest. The exaggerated rumour which led him to expect that all his sons were slain has prepared him for deriving some comfort from the real state of the case. The affair is not so terrible as first reported. "Only Amnon is dead." Absalom does not appear so guilty as first supposed.

And what now of Absalom? From the moment that his victim gave the last gasp, the lawless avenger feared the revenge of the princes and the people. "He was as much afraid of them, as they were of him. They fled from his malice, he from their justice." Not his sin caused him to flee, but the fear of punishment. He had long thought of the sin; had grown familiar with it; had craftily planned it, and he was not afraid of it. But he had not before weighed the penalty, nor realized a murderer's fate.

Often is it thus with those who violate any law of the land, or of God. They go into sin fear-lessly, or blindly, or passionately. They do not abhor the sin. They do not hate it because it is forbidden of God. They do not respect the law because they love righteousness. They delight in the sin, but after it is committed they begin to fear the punishment. The terrors of the law take hold upon them. They are sorry, not for the evil deed, but for the consequences. They flee from the scene of their crime, from the reach of human law, and often from the society where they are exposed. By their flight they condemn themselves.

We may imagine Absalom, lingering a moment on the borders of his estate, and asking himself, whither shall I flee? Where find protection? Home cannot give it. The camp of Joab cannot afford it. No safe hiding-place can be found among the mountains, for the avenger of blood may track him along the most secret paths. No cottage will shelter him, for the brand of Cain is burning on his brow. Ah, he may hide, but he cannot hide his sin, nor ward off the stroke of justice.

In this strait many a sinner finds himself. His crimes may not be so heinous in human eyes as Absalom's; his hands may not be dripping with blood, that cries from the ground for judgment, but his heart is stained, his conscience defiled, his life is forfeited before God. Whither shall he flee? Does he haste from the scene of his guilt? Memory drags it after him. From society? Conscience strikes at every step, and lashes him wherever he may rest. From God? It is impossible. The mountains falling upon him could not hide him from the kindled wrath of Jehovah. And the sinner often flees, like Absalom, as a fugitive from justice, but not as a refugee for mercy and liberty. Fear governs the fugitive; hope, the refugee.

Might not Absalom flee to a city of refuge? Hebron, the city of his birth, lay behind him. Not far distant was Shechem, and before entering it he might drink of Jacob's well. Toward the kingdom of his grandfather was Ramoth-Gilead. Why not flee to a refuge-city?

He must have known that there were such cities, with good roads thither, and their gates open to receive the man-slayer. He must have known the provisions of the law for all who came, panting and weary, and in fear, seeking their protection, unless he had lived as careless and regardless, as many a sinner now lives in wilful ignorance of the means and way of grace. God is a refuge, but many do not know the entrance to his high tower. Christ is a hiding-place, but they have not sought the door to his fold.

But Absalom knew that he had *no right* to an asylum in a city of refuge. The law secured protection only to one who had killed a person unawares, ignorantly, without enmity, or design. "But if he thrust him of hatred, or hurl at him by lying of wait, or in enmity smite him with his hand, that he die, he that smote him shall surely be put to death." Absalom's case, then, was desperate. The gates of a refuge city would prove the jaws of death, for he could claim no safety by right of law. And has any sinner a right to a refuge in God? Can he find salvation by right of law? Nay: the law condemns him to eternal death. And yet he may haste boldly into God's refuge, saying, "I flee unto thee to hide me." The law cannot save us, but Jesus is able to save even to the uttermost. The law condemns, but God, for Christ's sake, will forgive, and extend over us the broad shield of his merciful protection.

Nor had Absalom *any plea* to urge for mercy. There was no extenuation, of his crime. He could present nothing that would lessen the degree of his guilt, or lighten the deserved punishment. And can the sinner draw from his conduct, his intentions, or his circumstances, any plea that will avail before God? Can any argument drawn from his own life justify him? Is he not condemned by all things around and above him, and self-condemned by memory, by the conscience and by his own life? But yet the guiltiest sinner may flee to God's refuge. The more broken he is by confession, and the less he justifies or excuses himself, the more readily is he welcomed and provided with a full salvation. Yes, he may come boldly, saying,

Just as I am, without one plea,
But that thy blood was shed for me,
And that thou bidst me come to thee,
O Lamb of God I come.

Nor could Absalom find *any advocate* in a refuge-city, who would plead his cause with success. Should he flee thither, he must undergo a solemn trial, and make it appear that the homicide was not intentional, before he could find protection. None would there point to an atonement for his sins. None would appear as a substitute to die in

7

his stead. By no sacrifice could he be saved from the penalties of the law. And here, too, the refuge-cities come far short of a perfect type of Christ. He offers far more than they could afford. Jesus is the sinner's Advocate, and he may say "Whither shall I flee? Unto thee, O Christ, my only refuge. Many are my sins, but more abundant is thy atonement. I deserve to die, but thou, my Substitute, hast died for me. I hear thy voice in sweetest song; it commands me to hide in the clefts of the rock. Thou art that rock; its clefts are thy wounds, and there will I hide me from all the accusations of the world."

And if Absalom were within the gates of a refuge-city the avenger of blood might enter and demand him to be given up. and drag him thence to justice, or slay him without the walls. His sins were too great for it to shelter. Here also, the parallel, between the refuge-city and Christ, wholly fails. "None however guilty has been cast forth from the refuge which the cross of Christ affords." Nor will any ever be, for Jesus. who calls sinners to repentance, declares, "Him that cometh unto me, I will in no wise cast out." The heavier he feels the burden of his sins, the closer he may cling to the cross, where none ever perished. We have then a refuge, "in which the enemy, the accuser, has no power to enter, and whence his hand has no power to rend us. Christ is that refuge, and beyond all men upon whom the sun shines, are they happy who have taken sanctuary in him. Nothing from without can harm, nothing affright them more. They rest secure in him: and enfolded in his encircling arms, the storms which trouble the life of man, and sprinkle gray hairs here and there upon him, often before he knows it, affect him not in his quiet rest; or are heard only as the muttering thunders of the distant horizon, which only enhance his sense of safety, and do not trouble his repose. The house of his hope is not shaken, for it is founded on a rock." (Kitto.)

Absalom turned away from the city of refuge—that type of a sinner's hiding-place and safety in Christ Jesus. He fled to Geshur, whence his mother had come, and where his grandfather was more likely to praise than blame him for the deed that had brought upon him the fear of punishment. He was out of the kingdom, and beyond the reach of human law. But he could not—nor can any sinner—get beyond the territory where God reigns, nor throw himself out of the reach of the Divine law. He was not yet safe from a more dreadful justice than that of men. Geshur could afford no refuge for his soul. No human avenger might reach him, but still God was saying, "Vengeance is mine, I will repay."

One thing he might have done. It is what every guilty soul ought to do. He might have sought refuge in God. Though he seem angry, yet when the sinner, contrite for sin, and praying for pardon, boldly faces the deserved punishment, saying, "I can but perish if I go," he finds that anger turned away. Even though frowns veil his face, yet when the penitent one, in the boldness of his necessity for forgiveness, presses through the veil, he is met with the smiles and the light of a Father's countenance.

It was once asked of an eastern caliph, "If there were a great bow, vast in its curve as the arching sky, and the cord thereof reaching from the east to the west, and if God were the archer, and calamities the arrows, and men the objects at which they were shot, then to whom should the sons of men fly for protection?" The answer was, "The sons of men must fly unto the Lord." We cannot fly from the arrows of his justice, but when we turn to meet them, we shall find them withheld, and put back into the quiver, for Jesus has secured unto all his people the removal of the terrors of the law.

We are honouring Jehovah, and exalting his pardoning mercy, when we declare that even Absalom might have found forgiveness with God. He who forgave David when he confessed, "Against thee, thee only have I sinned," would have pardoned David's guiltier son, had he bowed in penitence and in faith. The chief of sinners may find forgiveness. This assurance, everywhere held out to us in God's word, has led many to seek Christ as the Permanent Refuge, whom they have found in the time of their trouble; He has hid them in his pavilion, in the secret of his tabernacle has he . hid them till their calamities were over-past; and they have experienced the great truth—that the door of mercy is closed in no man's face, that God's heart is shut against no man's misery, that God's hand is shut against no man's need, that God's eye is shut against no man's danger, that God's ear is shut against no man's prayer.

7 *

CHAPTER VI.

Absalom in Exile.

But doth the exile's heart securely there
In sunshine dwell?   Ah! when was exile blest?
When did bright scenes, clear heavens, or summer air
Chase from his soul the fever of unrest?

"Time and thinking tame the strongest grief."
This old proverb has in it far more of the worldly
than the Christian spirit.   It gives no intimation
of consolation in God.   Thinking could do little
for King David, when every thought of the tragedy
in his family opened afresh the wounds of his heart.
Time, at length, would give him something else to
think of, and thus very many now are partially
consoled. Poor comfort, but the best they have!
It is intimated that time had much to do in wearing
away the grief over the death of Amnon.   It might
in some measure heal the sorrows of David's heart.
But it could never silence the awful memories, nor
scare away the tragic dreams that would associate
themselves with the names of Amnon, Tamar, and
Absalom.   He knew well of a far better source of
comfort.   He knew that submission to the will of

God, though often the last, is always the best
means of consolation. "Thy will be done," is
often all that we can say, yet in truly saying it, we
are blessed with resignation.

Other anxieties, also, grew up in his mind,
crowding out the past sorrows. Three years had
passed since Absalom threw himself out of his father's protection and favour, and became an exile,
out-lawed and proscribed—three long years in
which David mourned for his wayward son every
day. "And the soul of King David longed to go
forth unto Absalom."

And why? First, he had a godly pity for his
absent son. Very sacred were these deep compassions. They were more than natural; they were
spiritual. How can the royal Psalmist touch his
harp, or sing a new song, when he has a son in a
heathen land, probably revelling and rioting at a
foreign court? Who wonders if he cannot feast,
and if tears are as his drink day and night? Who
can charm away his grief, if he break forth into
sighing, "O Absalom, my son, my son; how can I
give thee up, O Absalom?"

In every tender and generous heart, where the
feelings are purified in sorrow, we may find very
much that resembles the compassion of God. Especially is this found in the heart of David, the
theocratic representative of Jehovah. The Lord
delights to represent himself as a father, pitying
his children, and longing to go forth to them, even

when they are disobedient and rebellious. Here, then, in the depth of David's heart, we have some illustrations of the deep compassions of the Father above, still yearning for his wayward, wandering children, who are exiles from the Father's house, self-banished from the court of Heaven, and prodigals in a far country, wasting their substance and involving themselves in eternal ruin. How does he represent himself as grieved every day for those who have fled from his kingdom, and are estranged from his love! "I have nourished and brought up children, and they have rebelled against me. They have forsaken the Lord, they are gone away backward. Why should ye be stricken any more? Why revolt more and more? Is Ephraim my dear son? Is he a pleasant child? for since I spake against him I do earnestly remember him still: therefore my bowels are troubled for him: I will surely have mercy upon him."

Again: David's horror of Absalom's crime wore somewhat away. His sense of the outrage became less and less keen. The pendulum of his wrath that may have swung heavily against his favourite son, was slowly falling back the other way. All have noticed that if a criminal can lie in prison, ·and have his trial long delayed, the abhorrence of his crime lessens, and the indignation against him cools in the public mind. They who, at first, were almost ready to drag him from his cell, and lynch him, are now almost willing to open the doors and let him run at large; or if he be convicted and sentenced, they are quite willing to petition for his pardon. A proof, that if justice depended upon the mere feelings of men, it would not be duly administered. There would be too much haste and severity at the first, or at the last too great leniency and undeserved pity.

And here men often mistake in arguing from the human to the Divine. Because our sense of justice is influenced by our feelings, men imagine that God's compassion will, at length, prevail over his justice. They suppose that his hatred of sin will some time cool into the mildest complacency, and that he will finally lose all intention to punish the guilty in his pity for their souls. They seem to think that while his heart longs to go forth to them in their sinful exile, he will never execute the demands of his righteous and eternal government. They forget that time does not wear away the immutable justice of God, nor does mercy reduce it to an unmeaning attribute. They forget that his justice is not a merely human feeling, but a divine principle, growing ever stronger the more it is provoked. Never forget, that this compassionate Father is also a righteous Judge. And one reason why he pities, is, that the sinner is already exposed to the justice of his law. And the greatest manifestation of his love is seen in his sending his Son to deliver us from the law, which may be satisfied, but never repealed.

Also : David had been in exile, and knew its bitter experience. He remembered its trials, and therefore could feel deeply for his self-banished son. He had been driven by the revenge of Saul from the court, from the army, and across the borders of the kingdom. He had been a homeless wanderer, with scarcely an attendant ; in hourly dread of death, fain to beg a morsel of bread wherever he dare show his face, and often on the very brink of despair. No wonder he mourned every day for Absalom, because the court where his son was might be even worse than the wilds of the desert. In the wilderness of En-gedi, or in the land of Moab, David was not estranged from God, for he could say, "Because Thou hast been my help, therefore in the shadow of Thy wings will I rejoice." .But who would lead Absalom to say, "Thou art my refuge and my portion in the land of the living"?

And if David thus drew upon his experience for a large pity toward his exiled son, may we not think that the Son of God even now draws upon his past experience of our exile from the Father's house, and thus more fully realizes our condition? On this earth of ours he walked a homeless prophet, hungry and weary, hated of men and driven from their cities, hunted by persecutors and bent under human adversities, familiar with loneliness, and in the agonies of death exclaiming that he was, for a little, forsaken of God ; and may not he remember all that he once shared of our exile, when in heaven he is touched with the feeling of our infirmities, and is interceding for our restoration to the Father ? And how must he now look with compassion upon all who are like those on whom his eye of tender pity·fell when he once met them wandering still farther from God, or saw them fleeing away from him while he sought the lost ! They, of their own will, have gone astray like lost sheep, and are still straying farther in the wilderness. Not yet has he proclaimed a law forbidding their return. They have banished themselves, by their own sins, and can you wonder that Jesus pities, or that the soul of the Father longs to go forth unto them ?

Further: David must have had painful anxieties for Absalom, because he knew, by experience, the temptations of exile. His cherished son would be tempted to commit greater crimes, become more desperate, and bring upon himself accumulated woes.

David in his times of banishment, it must be confessed, had not strongly resisted and overcome temptation. He strangely and sinfully yielded. He was but human, when God permitted him to try his own strength. His was our weak nature, and what would we have done when thus tempted, desolate, dismayed ? Temptations must come powerfully to any one situated as David was, an outlaw, suspected everywhere, surprised often, waylaid and surrounded by enemies. His safety seemed to depend upon crafty policies, disguises, fraudulent expedients, and daring strategies. Of all these he had to repent, weeping bitterly. He was permitted to go just where thousands are perpetually going, to reveal to us the power of temptations, and to show unto all who come after, the only way of deliverance. He left us, printed in rock, the footsteps made when he returned again to his God with an overcoming faith.

But what would the faithless, lawless, Absalom do when tempted? Would he not make himself worse and worse in his exile? That was the pang daily entering his father's heart. His soul longed to go forth unto Absalom, that if it could not win him back, it might at least wreathe about his spirit the purifying remembrances of home; if it could not reform, it might restrain and curb him in his sadly directed career. He knew that the riotous prodigal would have full sweep in wickedness at Geshur's court.

Is not this the anxious fear of hundreds of parents who have sons away from home? Even the best places of study or employment have their temptations. Evil companions will surround them, like harpies, greedy to devour. Amusement and fashion may help to pave the way to ruin. And if they went out with the depraved heart of the prodigal, or of Absalom, there is no human power to hold them back from self-destruction. Nothing but the grace of God can save them.

Among all the parental anxieties there are none more intensely painful than those for a son who is running such a wreck. It is one of the things worse than death. Over the dead one may cease to mourn, as David ceased to mourn for Amnon, " seeing he was dead." But for the living there are daily compassions, ceaseless tears, and prayers. They have not yet finished their evil course. Something worse or better must be the result. And yet in the holiest parental heart, there is but a feeble intimation of what is in the heart of Jesus. He saw, when on earth, all our temptations in our exile from the throne and kingdom of the Father. And he now looks down with his all-pitying eye to see whether we resist them as he did in the wilderness, or yield to them as his people have sometimes done; and doth not his soul long.to go forth unto us ?

Partaker of the human name,
He knows the frailty of our frame.

Again: David must have had anxieties for the soul—the spiritual condition of Absalom. The exile was far from God. Even if his conscience were sometimes troubled by the mercies despised, or by his sins unacknowledged, yet he had no hope in God, to lift his spirit above the trials and temptations of banishment.

David knew, by experience, what it was to trust in the Lord, when in exile. The hunted wanderer was the object of Heaven's deepest interest and

8

affection. Often did he have a thorny pillow, an anxious mind, and a trembling heart. He wandered in the wilderness in a solitary way: he found no city to dwell in. Hungry and thirsty, his soul fainted in him. Then he cried unto the Lord in his trouble, and he delivered him out of his distresses. " God loves, as David knew," says old Christopher Ness, " to reserve his holy hand for a dead lift in behalf of his servants in covenant with him, when there is a damp upon their hopes, and a death upon their helps."

Thus if fear or folly drove David into exile, its experiences brought him nearer to God, and he became dearer to his heavenly Father. But was it thus with Absalom? There is not a gleam of evidence that he sought God in his estrangement. Without God, and without hope, he was heaping up judgments upon his soul. David must have felt only too sure of this, and can you wonder that his soul was consuming in its ardour to go forth unto him? The worse the son, the more anxiety for him.

There are thousands of fathers and mothers who understand this. Absent and wandering children are painfully remembered because they remain strangers to God—aliens from the commonwealth of Israel. It is not their bodily comfort that causes the deepest solicitude, for they may not be exposed to it. It is the soul's salvation for which they yearn. "If he were only a Christian," said a mother whose son was far distant in a land where every tongue was strange, and where every man that he met might prove a robber, "I could be comforted."

And it is the soul of the exiled sinner on which God fixes his anxieties. It was toward prodigals that Jesus directed his pity; over the Absaloms he mourned; over guilty Jerusalem he wept, and the burden of it all was, "They believe not on me."

David mourned and longed, pitied and, doubtless, prayed, but it seems that he did nothing more. He sent no message to Absalom. For three long years there was no entreaty, no invitation, no assurance that if he would return, penitent and obedient, he should be pardoned, and accepted again at home. Justice ruled the king. It was but just that his guilty son should remain forever banished. In all the mercies of the royal heart, there was nothing that could provide an atonement for Absalom's crime. The law demanded his death, and could the king invite his own son home to meet the retribution he deserved? Rather does he leave him to himself, still the object of a compassion powerless to save.

But not thus with our God. In his yearning love, he sends to us exiles, his words of entreaty, his messengers with kind invitations, and his Holy Spirit with his regenerating power. True it would have been just to leave us without a message or a call to return. But banished and lost as we are he sends even his only Son to seek and save. And in the riches of his compassion he provides an atonement. The Father is not inviting us to meet death at his throne, but to come to the cross and learn that Jesus died to secure us pardon and eternal life.

David's silence, however, was surely not from an unwillingness or an inability to forgive and restore the exiled son. There was an atonement for him, greater than any that the king could have devised. It was in the sacrifices offered upon the altars of the tabernacle—the holy types of the one great sacrifice to be offered in due time on Calvary. God had the dispensing power to forgive all his sins, and David as king, could have reprieved the sentence of the law. Let him return in penitence, vowing at the altars his allegiance to God and the king; let him seek the pardon of the heavenly and the earthly father, and he might be welcomed with joy in Jerusalem, and with hallelujahs in heaven.

Did not Absalom know this? Yet he shut out the recollections, the motives, and the mercies, that would have led him to repentance. He was too haughty to accept of peace and reconciliation on such terms. He was utterly averse to confession and prayer, humiliation and amendment, pledges and vows to God. The great hatred of his heart was against God and holiness. No gospel would he accept, no sacrifice would he acknowledge, no atonement would he receive, no reformation of life, nor change of heart would he seek. He wished no restoration that must begin with God, and if in his exile there were tears, it was not the weeping of penitence. If there were sorrows, they were not godly sorrows that work repentance.

Absalom might have found forgiveness through the sacrifices on the altar; we may find it through Christ on Calvary. If we had nothing to preach to men but God's compassions, it must be a hopeless message to the hearers; but we preach Christ crucified—a sacrifice for sins—a Saviour for sinners. The Father not only longs for the lost, but provides every needed means for their recovery, and now waits for their return. Rise, and go to thy Father!

He is saying, " Return, ye backsliding children, and I will heal your backslidings." Shall not we respond, " Behold, we come unto thee, for thou art the Lord our God?"

8 *

CHAPTER VII.

The Hand of Joab.

Young men soon give, and soon forget affronts ;
Old age is slow in both.

DAVID in his shepherd-days may have climbed
the mountains that rose near Bethlehem, and looked
off upon the town that lay upon the slopes of Mount
Moriah, and wondered at the strength of the for-
tress that crowned it. Perhaps he knew the tradition that to that very mountain Abraham had
once led his son Isaac for the intended sacrifice.
But he did not foresee that he would one day make
of that town Jerusalem the joy of the earth, where
the tribes would assemble, whence prophets should
go forth, and out of whose gate the Messiah would
be led to be crucified on Calvary.

When David became the acknowledged king of
all Israel, one of his greatest enterprises was to
capture Jerusalem from the Jebusites, who then
held it in defiance of his power. He besieged it, and
the voice of derision rang from the citadel, in contempt of the forces that were pitched near the

walls. In order to fire the ardour of his brave soldiers, he promised that the man who should first break through the walls, should have the post of chief-captain in the army.

There was one man, ambitious, bold, crafty, rude, and sometimes reckless, to whom this was no idle offer. He attempted the perilous feat, surprising the garrison, and taking the strong-hold, probably, in something of the style of Ethan Allen at Ticonderoga, who, when asked, "By whose authority do you come?" replied with an oath and a flourish of his sword, "In the name of the Great Jehovah, and the continental congress!" This man was Joab, a nephew of the king.

Bravery, in human eyes, often atones for the want of high moral principle and upright conduct. It was well known that Joab had been impetuous, unscrupulous, and revengeful. Already had he proved lawless in the murder of Abner, and a dangerous man in the use of military power. The king found it hard to curb him, and was obliged to say of him, especially among his sister's sons, "I am this day weak, though anointed king; and these men, the sons of Zeruiah, be too hard for me: the Lord shall reward the doer of evil according to his wickedness." By careful policy, Joab had held a high position, and now his daring exploit won for him a higher promotion. David gave him the chief command, and entrusted to him some of the weightiest affairs of the administration.

Still the rough, bold-tempered chief was closely watched. He knew it. Not always very ceremonious, and never a cringing servant willing to loose his master's shoe-latchet for a favour, yet he was careful to let his life run smoothly with that of his king. Independent, intrepid, and full of military pride, he added greatly to the security and glory of the kingdom. In character he was a Marlborough, without his public and ruinous mistakes; in generalship a Wellington, without his solid virtues. In all the policies of the War-office, David soon learned how to detect the hand of Joab.

The hand of Joab, moved by the heart of his king, had much to do in an event that brought severe judgments upon the house of David. It was to this iron nerved commander that the order was given, "Set Uriah in the fore-front of the hottest battle." The plot succeeded. Uriah was slain. Two of the blackest crimes of the decalogue now provoked Jehovah's anger, and hence calamitous judgments were preparing for David. "Now, therefore, the sword shall never depart from thine house," and when those blackest crimes re-appeared intensified in his own family he began to realize the terrible predictions of the faithful prophet.

And now the hand of Joab appears again. The wily general can see that something is the matter with his king. Perhaps David had lately seemed often abstracted, forgetful, neglectful: gave strange orders in the military department; hardly knew

what he was doing in the civil administration;
planned no great enterprises for three years; failed
to do certain things, and did some things twice; appeared singular at the court; was nervous at the
council, and was evidently breaking down under
some great sorrow. Joab detected what was a
great part of the trouble—"The king's heart was
toward Absalom." He, probably, saw too that
the hearts of the people were strongly turned in
the same direction, for the public indignation had
softened into pity; and what the king longed for,
and the people wished, was quite sure to be ef-
fected before very long. Therefore, thinking it
well to have the credit of bringing about a popular
result, he took the matter resolutely in hand.

A practical subject may here be illustrated, viz;
*Peace attempted upon wrong terms and by false me-
thods.* Notice, *First,* the wrong kind of peace
sought for the exiled Absalom. Joab devises it.
He does not consult the law, to know what its demands are; nor the judges, to get their terms for
the restoration of a criminal; nor the government,
to find its pardoning power; nor the king, to learn
what conditions he may offer. The question is not,
" How can Absalom's sin be atoned and pardoned,
and he be first reformed, and then restored;" but
rather, " How can a peace—any sort of a peace—
be brought about?" And thus he attempts the
slight healing of a deep wound, not on principles
of right, but by a temporizing policy. He will

whisper peace, peace. and deceive the king into
measures which ignore or annul the righteous laws
of his kingdom. He stands in the lead of those
who would contrive to effect a temporary peace between the sinner and his God. In no little theology one may detect the hand of Joab.

One would suppose that Joab would have made
a petition to the king, interceded for Absalom's
pardon, and prepared the way for his return.
Then, knowing the largeness of David's compassions, would have gone to the exile, taught him repentance, tried to move his heart and melt his soul
by the remembrances of his father's tenderness
and great mercy. We look for him to haste to
Geshur, and there plead with the wanderer, en-
treating him, by all the meekness, gentleness and
sure mercies of David, to pray God that his sin
might be forgiven in heaven, and thus be also forgiven on earth; and even with tears imploring him
not to further aggravate the wounds of his father's
heart, nor bring him down in sorrow to a prema-
ture grave. We look for the hand of Joab, leading the exile back, penitent, and almost overcome
by the prospect of such reconciliation and peace,
and then at the throne we expect to hear Joab interceding in behalf of the guilty prince. But no!
that hand is craftily forming another scheme, and
preparing mischief that will cause the throne to
shake, and all Israel to feel the shock.

What a mediator he might have been!—a type

of our Lord, who undertook the work of reconciling us to the God whose laws we had violated; to the Father whose compassions we abused, and to the King from whose spiritual kingdom we had fled, seeking shelter in a world of exile and of earthly woe. For our Mediator first obtained from the Father his terms of peace. He consulted the demands of the law upon us, and proposed to satisfy them. Then he came to us, entreated us by all the love of God, and besought us with tears and sufferings to return to the Father's house. He gave himself unto death to make clear the way for our reconciliation, and having ascended from the grave, he ever liveth to make intercession for us.

Secondly. Notice the ingenious method of securing a false peace. If anything· could touch the king's heart, it was poetry and parable, whose glowing words would warm his imagination, and kindle the noblest impulses of his soul. Nathan knew this when he wished to bring his king to repentance. Argument might fail, but the parable of the poor man, from whom was rudely torn the one little lamb that was to him as a daughter, would surely prove effective. And so it did. Joab, doubtless, knew that his king could thus be moved; and he knew, too, that a bad cause and a false argument may be made to appear well by a deceptive illustration. Error is often made to look like truth by dressing it in striking imagery. Deceit-

ful illustrations are ever dangerous, blurring the
intellect, and rousing the sympathies. Of themselves, they never prove anything, but they may
blind you to the falsity of an evil doctrine, and the
weakness of a bad argument. Here then is Joab's
strategy. He cannot gain his bad cause by cool
argument, but he may succeed by a delusive
parable.

On a day when the king is in one of his better
moods a woman of Tekoah appears, as a widow,
disconsolate, and troubled for a son who, in his unfortunate rashness, slew his brother in the field.
And now the whole circle of her friends has risen
to avenge the blood of the slain. She asks that
her son may be protected, so that the family name
may not be extinguished, like the quenching of the
last coal* upon a widow's hearth.

David listens, but is not yet touched. He does
not yet see the point, nor make the application to
himself. Is he wary of parables now, since the
arrow of conviction was shot into his heart by the
prophet Nathan? It seems but a plain matter of
fact; he will see the proper authorities, and have
justice done to her son. Not a hair of his head
shall fall to the earth.

Now follows the imagery that captures the mind

---

* That was certainly a very strong figure, well adapted to turn
David's mind to the law which might secure the protection of her
pretended son. Plato called those who escaped Deucalion's flood,
"The few live coals of the human race."

of the king. "And the woman said, Wherefore then hast thou thought such a thing against the people of God? [as that they demand the life of thy son:] for the king doth speak this thing as one which is faulty, in that the king doth not fetch home again his banished. For we must needs die, and are as water spilt on the ground, which cannot be gathered up again; neither doth God respect any person; yet doth he devise means that his banished be not expelled from him."

"Is not the hand of Joab in all this?" exclaims David, carried away by sympathy, by an imagination, by a deception. And yet having committed himself, he cannot retract; not if Absalom may have the benefit of the delusion. He orders Joab to bring him home.

The fallacy in her story is, that the king was under obligation to "fetch home his banished," without requiring any satisfaction to a just law: and that God will bring home his banished without any terms of reconciliation. It is true, however, that "God doth devise means that his banished be not expelled from him." He has given his word, his Son, his Spirit, his church and all its ordinances, so that we may have abundant means and motives to return and be at peace with him.

Thirdly, Notice the delusiveness of a wrong method of peace. Absalom is brought back to Jerusalem, expecting probably that his father will hasten to meet him, fall on his neck, weep, welcome,

9

and forgive.   But no ! he finds nothing of the sort.
There is no way of justification provided for him,
no access to his father's presence, no liberty, no
reconciliation, no pardon, no peace at all.   The
king has said. " Let him turn to his own house, and
let him not ,see my face."   This favour of home
and family is more than most rulers would have
allowed to a guilty subject, or even to a criminal
son.

" That he was not admitted into the king's presence," remarks Dr. Kitto, " was a sign well understood, far more significantly in the East than it
would be even with us, that he was still under disgrace.   It in fact compelled him to live as a private person, and to lead a retired life ; for it would
have been outrageously scandalous for him to have
appeared in public, or to have assumed any state,
until he appeared at court.   The courtiers were
also constrained to avoid him."

He is a guilty man, still impenitent, and must
not be deluded with the false notion that forgiveness is so cheap, that it is a mere gratuity to be
tossed to every criminal and every rebel without
regard to any satisfaction to the law, or any allegiance to the government.   He must know that he
still deserves the full penalties of justice.   Pardon
is justly withheld, and access denied ; his house is
deservedly made a sort of prison, beyond whose
walls he must not go.   Banishment was hard, but
imprisonment is harder to endure.

And more: he is a dangerous man. One who could slay a brother in cold blood must be dangerous. One who could murder the heir-apparent to the throne to clear the way for himself must be dangerous. One who could already show signs of plotting to overthrow the government, must be a man of treacherous intentions, worthy of "durance vile." It is not safe for him to run at large and undermine the national liberties. And what respect or obedience can be paid to David's administration if he give so guilty and dangerous a man his freedom unrestrained? Absalom has forfeited his right to liberty, and therefore is not wronged by the judicious confinement.

And did you never think that if such a peace were extended to impenitent sinners, and they were received into heaven, they would be dangerous courtiers about the throne of God? They never repented of their sins; they may commit them still. They never were changed in heart; they may prove as debased and corrupting as ever before. They never disavowed their rebellion against God's holy government; they may show themselves again rebellious. They never vowed their allegiance to heaven's King; they may plot conspiracy and raise revolt against his authority. Satan did it once, and they may follow his example. They would endanger the happy obedience of saints and angels, for how could the holiest beings in heaven fully reverence and serve their King

if he tolerated among them the impenitent, the un-
pardoned, the unregenerate? Nay, this can never
be, for the fearful, and the abominable, and whosoever loveth and maketh a lie, must be excluded
from the kingdom of God. He, in justice, will
turn every such sinner to his own place, never to
see his face in peace.

" So Absalom dwelt two full years in Jerusalem,
and saw not the king's face." You ask, Even if this
were just, was it not an unwise policy? What
good could it do? What evil it might bring about?
It would draw to Absalom the sympathies of the
people. They do not like to see these sudden ar-
rests by the government, and these imprisonments,
however dangerous the men are supposed to be.
They are likely to imagine that such a man is suffering only from suspicion or jealousy. They may
make a political martyr of him, and by the magic
of the name of their most princely Absalom, may
gather a party in opposition to the administration.
How they will recall the handsome prince of such
courtly bearing and winning address! How his
absence on state occasions would only cause them
to think and speak of him the more! It would be
deemed very hard, that the now apparent heir to
the throne,* who could grace any procession, and
any festivity, should never be seen, save in the

---

* Chileab the second son of David was probably dead, and Solomon, much younger than Absalom, was perhaps not indicated, and
certainly not publicly known as the successor to the throne.

guarded enclosures of his private dwelling. Then was not his confinement very impolitic?

We answer that it was not mere state policy that induced the king to treat his son with such rigour. Nor was it his delight in the display of arbitrary power. It was principle. It was a necessity imposed by justice as well as by safety. For Absalom was not only a guilty and a dangerous man, but he was a desperate man. He was designing and unscrupulous. His record proved it. Perhaps in his exile he had given some proof that he was there plotting a scheme of rebellion, and David was glad to have him more completely in his power. You cannot believe, for one moment, that the king, with all his excessive tenderness and favouritism toward his son, would have so dealt with him, unless he had the best of reasons and justice on his side.

Still you ask, What would be the effect on Absalom's spirit and temper? How would he like to hear of festivals, and public rejoicings, when all but himself were present? How brook the rumour that ambassadors from the surrounding courts were being paraded through Jerusalem, and he alone excluded from their society? So fond of exhibiting his fine appearance, how endure to be forbidden his imposing displays?

No doubt his spirit was chafed, and his mind dismally clouded. No doubt he felt exasperated, and thought of revenge. But it was his fault rather

9 *

than his misfortune, and the fault was his own—
not David's. And the fact that he was exasperated, was the best reason why he should be held
under close restraint. The fact that this lion
chafes and roars only proves that he still deserves
the iron band and guarded cage. Let him loose,
and he will make terrible havoc of life and liberty.

But you say, Punishment will not reform nor
tame him into allegiance. Grant it. This is just
why he needs the punishment. If one does not reform under it, he deserves it all the more. If re-
leased he would be the same man still. And remember that punishment is not designed mainly
for the reformation of the criminal, but for the
sake of justice, law, and government. The question is not, Will he be made better by it? But,
Does he deserve it for his crimes? On this principle God punishes men, and delegates to the proper
authorities the right to punish transgressors of the
law. Nor does reformation secure the right to be
set free from the penalties of justice.

"Three years," writes Matthew Henry, "Absalom had been in exile with his grandfather, and
now two years a prisoner at large in his own house,
and in both better dealt with than he deserved ;
yet his spirit was still unhumbled, his pride unmor-
tified, and instead of being thankful that his life is
spared, he thinks himself sorely wronged that he is
not restored to all his places at court. Had he
truly repented of his sin, his distance from the

gayeties of the court, and his solitude and confinement in his own house would have been very agreeable to him. If a murderer must live, let him be
for ever a recluse. But Absalom cannot bear this
just and gentle mortification; he longs to see the
king's face, pretending it was because he loved
him, but really because he wanted an opportunity
to supplant him. He cannot do his father mischief till he is reconciled to him; this therefore is
the first branch of his plot; this snake cannot
sting again till he be warmed in his father's
bosom."

Absalom feels that his is but an unsatisfactory
peace. He must have access to his father, and
therefore we have another phase of the subject.

Fourthly, Notice the unjust and imperious dic-
tates of a peace attempted upon wrong terms and
by ingenious methods. He proposes to gain his
point, "not by pretended submissions and promises of reformation, but (would you think of it?)
by insults and injuries." He has evidently demanded that he may see his father. He has it in
mind to dictate his own terms of reconciliation, and
David knows, too well, the only terms of a righteous peace with God, to let his son make the conditions on which he shall be restored. His love for
the prince has made his severity towards him very
painful to his heart, and he is entitled to much credit for his self-restraint.

It seems that Joab has, by this time, fully con-

sented to the justice of Absalom's treatment. He
employs no more parables, no further craftiness.
He ceases to go near the unforgiven prince. Again
and again does Absalom send for the wily and rug-
ged general, but in vain. Joab does not come.

We are quite amused at the plan adopted to
bring Joab near him. It could not be more cunning and effective, proving that adversity sharp-
ened his wit, if it did not put an edge upon his
conscience. It is for the servants, on the estate
of the prince, to set Joab's neighbouring field of
barley on fire. They do it, and this brings him in
hot haste, and with keen rebuke. Then Absalom
makes his demands, in his own name, and with the
assumption of authority. He requests instant
death, or unconditional pardon from his father.

"Say to the king, Wherefore am I come from
Geshur? It had been good for me to have been
there still! Now therefore, let me see the king's
face; and if there be any iniquity in me, let him
kill me."

What! does he pretend to doubt whether there
be any iniquity in him? And dare to insinuate
that he is guiltless? And intimate that he is un-
justly treated? And to demand that his innocence
recommend him to the royal favour? There are
no confessions, no entreaties for pardon; no pledges
of loyalty to the king; nothing but insolence, and
a fling at his father's severity. Ah! the unsatisfactory peace already granted, has only deluded

him into a false notion of his rights, and filled him
with proud dictation to his sovereign. Strange are
such demands; but not more strange than those
which sinners make, when, deluded by a mere temporary peace, they come at last to claim admission
into God's presence and glory, without prayer,
without confession or pledge, and only with self-
righteousness, and a pretension to the rewards of
innocence. Yes, even with a complaint that longer
punishment for their sin, is unjust and undeserved.
Thus do men abuse the forbearance and long-suffering of God, who withholds a deserved severity, that
they may have space for repentance.

The demands are unjust, yet David relents when
the bold general pleads for Absalom. Perhaps he
fears the effect of longer keeping the young prince
under such restrictions, for those who sympathize
with the public favourite may be excited to conspire against the throne. But more likely, he cannot resist the appeal to his tenderness and love.
His better judgment yields to the promptings of
his heart. For five years he has not seen his once
indulged son. For two years he has been almost
within hearing of his voice, and yet not a word
has passed. As Joab pleads, the king gives
way. He is imposed upon by the very boldness
of his son's request, and blind to the motives that
prompt it. He suspects not the worst that may
come; he hopes for the best. Justice shall be set
aside. The law against murder shall be for once

suspended or overlooked. The criminal need not
be penitent. The danger of his over-riding all
government shall be dismissed. The securities for
obedience shall not be demanded. Absalom shall
see the king's face.   .

Had there been true repentance in the son, as
he came to his father, the scene of their meeting
would have its only parallel in the case of the prodigal son, when his father saw him while yet a
great way off, and ran, and fell on his neck, and
kissed him, and heard his confession, but would not
hear his tearful plea to be made one of his hired
servants, and at once gave him the fullest assurance that he was perfectly restored to his father's
house and heart. But there is not a word here
about weeping at the gate, nor of robe or ring, nor
of feasting in the halls, nor of rejoicing in the palace. Only this—when David "called for Absalom, he came to the king, and bowed himself on his
face to the ground before the king; and the king
kissed Absalom."

Was it the kiss of peace? Was it forgiveness?
Was it full reconciliation? It seems rather a mere
toleration; a cessation of penalties; a suspension
of severities, which David, in his profound sense
of justice, knew to be deserved. Yet an experiment might be made of leniency. There is nothing
of what we find in the formal pardon extended to
Charles the Bold of Burgundy, after he had offended his father, and been refused admittance

into his presence. The old Duke once "snatched up a weapon, and, tottering from his chamber, vowed to take vengeance on his son." But persuasive words disarmed his impotent fury, and at length by various ingenuities an appeal was made for peace. The son was introduced with greater outward pomp than inward penitence, by the Joabs of the court, and he made his defensive confession. Philip the Good heard it, and then raising him up, kissed him, saying, "Charles, my son, I pardon all the offences you have ever committed against me to the present hour; be my good son, and I will be your good father." The lips that kissed Absalom seem to have been dumb, and if there fell a tear it was one of pity rather than of joyful pardon.

In all this there is very much that may be applied to show the difference between a sincere desire and a selfish desire for the favour of God, our rightful king and merciful Father. "Absalom felt it an evil to be on bad terms with his father, but he felt neither hatred nor sorrow for the sin that caused him to be so." He only hated the results of that sin upon his earthly condition. "He desired to be reinstated in his father's favour, simply because he could not otherwise compass his selfish projects. What he desired was the good things of the kingdom, not the fellowship of the king; his own selfish interests, not the honour or glory of his father. So there are men that desire to be at peace with God, not because they esteem and love him, for his infinite goodness and excellence, but solely because they are alarmed for their own personal welfare. * * It is true, indeed, that concern for personal safety in eternity is often the starting-point of a genuine religious career." It was so in the case of the Philippian jailer, and the thousands who asked on the day of Pentecost, "Men and brethren what shall we do?" But if it be the starting-point, it is certainly not the goal. There is always suspicion when a man's religion amounts only to a concern for his welfare hereafter.

King David knew full well that there is no forgiveness, or peace with God without repentance; none without faith in the sacrifice that secures atonement for the sinner. Faith in God brought him peace, for he was justified, and delivered from the penalties of the law which he had violated. And not only peace, but access to the king of glory; and rejoicing in the hope of the glory of God he could say, "Blessed is the man whom thou causest to approach unto thee, that he may dwell in thy courts." Blessed is he, who in penitence and faith can say, "Make Thy face to shine upon thy servant; save me for thy mercies' sake."

And if we would ever see the King's face, and dwell near his throne, where angels are the ministers, and the saints are the princes of the Most High, let us be first justified by faith, then we shall have peace with God, and access through our Lord

Jesus Christ. We shall be sons in his house, heirs of his kingdom, and shall reign with our Lord for ever and ever.

> Return, O wanderer, return,
>   Thy Saviour bids thy spirit live;
> Go to his bleeding feet and learn,
>   How freely Jesus can forgive.

10

CHAPTER VIII.

Absalom Plotting Treason.

Treason is there in its most horrid shape,
Where trust is greatest! and the soul resigned,
Is stabbed by her own guards.

UNDER the king's kiss the traitor prepares to
stab. As soon as Absalom is admitted to the
court, he begins to act so badly that worse may
seem impossible. Ingratitude can do no more:
treason aims at nothing less. If his rebellion surprises us, it does not surprise him. In heart and
mind he is no stranger to it. His whole life has,
evidently, been an advance toward the great crime
against just government, which God has clearly
marked with his displeasure.

Absalom's first rebellion was against God. How
early the symptoms of it appeared, we know not,
but we do know that in the earliest years one may
disobey the laws, and shake off the authority of
heaven's King. The after life may prove an early
want of allegiance to Jehovah. The sooner the
child becomes loyal to God, the surer is he to become obedient unto the "powers that be" on earth.

and unto him who ordained them for the good of men.

His next rebellion was against the laws of home. Doubtless he started up prematurely to be his own master, and set up a government for himself. Many a traitor and conspirator was in childhood a little rebel, opposing, with all his might, the parental authority and rules. The mother of Benedict Arnold was a woman of exemplary piety, and the parental government was the kindest, but "the child was father of the man." He was perverse from the beginning. He loved the malicious sort of mischief. Applause delighted him, and if he could not win praise by daring deeds, he made himself notorious by boyish lawlessness. As a man, treason has made him infamous. So Aaron Burr. What the widowed and saintly mother wrote of her little son, would, very likely, have applied to Absalom in his young days. "Most say that he is handsome, but not so good-tempered. He is very resolute, and requires a good governor to bring him to terms." This child was often in a state of rebellion. When four years old he refused submission to his tutor, and ran away : at ten he made another like experiment, and the only biographer who has attempted to whiten his character says that the "little stories" of his boyhood " exhibit the rebel merely"—the rebel against the laws of home.

The third rebellion of Absalom was against the

laws of society, and of the land. And here he
may be classed with Aaron Burr, who casting his
shadow before, wrote, as if by prophecy, during
his college life, his own wreck, and its cause.
"The passions, if properly regulated, are the
gentle gales which keep life from stagnating; but
if let loose, they become the tempests which tear
everything before them. Do we not frequently
behold men of the most sprightly genius, by giving
loose reins to their passions, lost to society, and
reduced to the lowest ebb of misery and despair?
Do we not frequently behold persons of the most
penetrating discernment, and happy turn for polite
literature, by mingling with the sons of sensuality
and riot, blasted in all the bloom of life?" Yes,
indeed, we do! and thine own speech bewrayeth thee.
By shaking off the best of social laws, thou makest
thyself the very man whom thou hast portrayed!

All this is not enough for Absalom. He is plotting a fourth rebellion—one against the national
government. Scarce has the impress of his father's
kiss left him, when he is earnestly engaged in this
nefarious business of treason. There are several
things that aggravate his conduct in scheming a
rebellion.

It is plotted in the capital—at the court. If
seeing the king's face means that he is admitted
into the king's councils,* then he is in the very cab-

* "To see the king's face, that is, to become a privy counsellor,"
says Matthew Henry, citing Esther i. 14, where reference is made to

inet hatching rebellion, and, while professing allegiance, is making the largest preparation for the overthrow of the government. Cataline, even while conspiring against the Roman state, trod the streets of the capital defiant of the grasp of justice, and had the boldness to take his seat in the senate, and listen to the scathing denunciations of Cicero. Absalom need not be so bold, for where a Cataline would mount the walls, he mines under them.

It is a dangerous policy—a bad precedent. May he not fail against the king whom Jehovah has placed upon the throne? And even if he succeed, may not some one rise up against him, betray, rebel, and rob him of his crown? What he gains by treason may he not lose by treason? And what an example will he be to all his successors! It is a remarkable fact, that after the secession of the ten tribes, so many of their kings rose and fell by such conspiracies.

It is a daring, desperate policy. God has established the government against which he plots. It is a theocracy. David is the vicar of God upon the throne. To conspire against it, is to conspire against the throne of Jehovah, and to run the terrible risk of having to contend with the Almighty. For ourselves, we have reason to heed the words

certain persons, "which saw the king's face, and which sat the first in the kingdom." We cannot be certain, however, that Absalom held this position.

10 *

of St. Paul, "Let every soul be subject unto the higher powers. For there is no power but of God; the powers that be are ordained of God. Whosoever, therefore, resisteth the power, resisteth the ordinance of God; and they that resist shall receive to themselves damnation." •

Absalom's scheme is a godless one. It is an anti-religious and infidel movement. We cannot hold rebellion in too great abhorrence, as a sin against God and true religion.

> Rebellion ! foul dishonouring word,
>   Whose wrongful blight so oft has stained
> The holiest cause that tongue or sword
>   Of mortal ever lost or gained.
> How many a spirit born to bless
>   Hath sunk beneath that withering name
> Whom but a day's, an hour's success
>   Had wafted to eternal fame.

There is reason to think that, at this time, there was in the Hebrew nation a strong element of ungodliness. The occasional outbursts of enthusiasm and patriotism were not sure evidences of piety. There is a lonely tone in many of the Psalms, as if king David felt that his devotion to God brought him into solitude. In his court he wanted congenial company. There was no heavenly balm in the breath of men around him. The irreligious Joab was his chief general. No Havelock was in the army. The ungodly Ahithophel was his chief counsellor. A deep under-current of dislike to the piety of David seemed to pervade the nation, and only waited for Absalom to raise the flood-gates, when it would become a torrent, carrying all before it with a sweeping destruction. Such a villainous movement could not have had the vast support which it received, if even the tribe of Judah had possessed a firmly-settled piety. We cannot think much of the piety of a people who are so ready to rise up against a good government, and against such a ruler as David. And had Absalom been successful, scenes might have occurred similar to those of the French Revolution, which originated with infidels who sought to consummate their schemes by overturning the government, desecrating the altars of the church, and declaring that religion was banished from the realm.

It is also a heartless scheme. What! Absalom conspire against his own father! and such a father! indulgent almost to excess, compassionate to a fault, and delighting in his son with a favouritism that astonishes us. How can he dare to rob his father of his crown and of his life? Is he prompted only by an ambition to rule, or is he coolly seeking revenge for the banishment and disgrace so lately endured? We cannot say that he from the first designs to take his father's life, but "generally, that which aims at the crown, aims at the head that wears it."

Nor is this all. There is no cause for Absalom's conspiracy. Not a shadow of just complaint can he bring against the government, or the present

administration. He does not represent a people
over-ridden and oppressed. Not a word comes
from them; not one cry for the redress of their
grievances; not one plea for rights of which they
have been deprived; not a protest against misrule,
nor a petition for reform. It is not a people's movement. It is the work of one man, and he the indulged Absalom, who ought to be the most grateful
and loyal subject in the kingdom. Never did Israel have so good a government; never was it better administered than by David; never were the
people more prosperous, more contented, and more
happy, until this rebellious prince artfully deludes
them into dissatisfaction by his utterly false persuasions.

Where can any motive be found for his conduct?
We must give Absalom the credit of a quick per-
ception. He can easily see that his chances are
not the brightest for his being the heir and successor to the throne in a peaceable way. He may be
the oldest living son, but that does not insure to
him the succession. He has forfeited every claim
that he may bring forward by his crimes. There
is no precedent to favour him. No one has yet
succeeded to the throne by the right of being the
oldest son. David is but the second king, and he
is not a son of the first. Jonathan was set aside
for him. The crown may pass out of the present
royal family by the appointment of God, especially
as Absalom is so unworthy. He knows that he is

not fit for it. Or David may exercise the dispensing power, and appoint whom he considers best qualified to the throne. Poor hope for Absalom on this ground! He may be "second to no one in his father's heart, but enough has passed to satisfy him that he holds no high place in his father's judgment." Besides all this, he may be aware that the successor is already pointed out. Solomon is fourteen years of age, and David may already have said to Bath-sheba, "Assuredly Solomon thy son shall reign after me, and he shall sit upon my throne in my stead." If Absalom knows of this promise, we can see some motive for him to hasten and seize the crown before his brother shall be strong enough to frustrate his ambition. If he does not know it, he can see enough to make his prospects in the future very precarious. To wait for his father's death in the order of providence will be quite certain to defeat his hopes. The only sure way is the short one; and that short way is treason.

Give him credit for perceiving this, for it is hard to find anything creditable in him. It proves that he was no fool, but it also makes him the greater knave. For what right had he to the throne? He was not the first-born. The eldest brother had fallen a victim to his revenge, if not to his ambition for the royal power. God only intended him for a prince, and had qualified him to be a good one, by the most generous endowments. And why

not be what God intended? Why seek a station
that Providence never designed? Why is any man
unwilling to be just what God has fitted him to be?

> It is the curse of mighty minds oppressed,
> To think what their state is, and what it should be;
> Impatient of their lot, they reason fiercely,
> And call the laws of Providence unequal.

It has been well said that "the liberty to go
higher than we are, is only given when we have
fulfilled the duty of our present sphere. Thus men
are to rise upon their performances, and not upon
their discontent."

CHAPTER IX.

Stealing Hearts.

Smooth runs the water, where the brook is deep,
And in his simple show he harbours treason.
The fox barks not when he would steal a lamb.

ABSALOM must have means to carry out his rebellious scheme, and hence he committed one great robbery. Not that of rifling the royal treasuries, nor that of securing to himself the best weapons of war; but he "stole the hearts of the men of Israel." Stole them from his father. If he could gain their admiration, their confidence, their affection, and their enthusiasm, then he might be sure of all else—money, arms, warriors. The king would be left desolate. He would have the nation, and of course the throne. This, then, was the first thing to be done, and to it he gave his whole mind and heart. He brought into play every accomplishment, every artifice, and every energy. There was nothing to which he would not stoop in order to conquer. Every wire must be worked; every popular fancy gratified, that he may "sit high in all the people's hearts."

He turned his personal beauty to his advantage. Even when under disgrace and a state prisoner in his own house, he seems to have cultivated the arts that would give him a fine appearance. A glimpse of him through the lattice or half-shut gate might strike some passer-by with admiration and pity. At that time he had the distinction, such as it is, of being the handsomest young man of his day. "In all Israel there was no one so much to be praised as Absalom for his beauty; from the sole of his foot even to the crown of his head, there was no blemish in him." Had there been anything else good about him, this would have been well enough. God gave him this beauty: none should despise the rare gift. But he doted upon it, as is clearly hinted in the attention that he gave to his toilette. Notice is taken of his hair, not as that of a Nazarite, for he was far from such strictness, but as that of a dandy. He did not dream that "his hair was to be his halter," nor could he have failed to take the highest offence at a rebuke like that of a far later day, "Doth not even nature itself teach you, that if a man have long hair, it is a shame unto him?" The mystery of its weight, would lead us into a long discussion about shekels, unguents, gold-dust, modes and times of "polling," and the possible change of one Hebrew letter for another very like it, by some copyist, so that instead of "two hundred shekels," the original record was four shekels. The average crop reaped, or the annual burden, was somewhere near four or five pounds, taking the locks, ointment and powder all together. Much or little, Absalom attached such importance to it, that he gloried in it until it "was heavy on him," and then weighed it so that even in his loss he might have some satisfaction. All this may seem trifling to us, but trifles reveal character. We may infer from this one thing, his devotion to dress and ornament. It has been said that "he was at the court of David what George IV. was to England in his day—the handsomest man, and at the same time of least account, in all the kingdom." He was the leader of fashion: the foppish gentleman of the times: the Chesterfield in Jerusalem, and the Beau Nash of all Israel. "None but himself can be his parallel."

He thus attracted public attention. By gaining the people's eyes, he was in a fair way to steal their hearts. Much could be done to overcome the contempt of his foppery, by his engaging manners, his avowed interest in everybody, and his professed sympathies coming from a heart, apparently, the most frank, open, and generous. And the people had one reason to praise his beauty, which we may not so readily appreciate as they did. The lamb to be laid upon the altar must be "without blemish," and also the priest who offered it, and they seem to have considered the same bodily excellence as quite essential to the possessor of the throne. In the case of Saul, his eminent stature contributed

11

very much to his nomination and acceptance by the
people; and in the appointment of David no little
stress is laid upon the fact that "he was ruddy,
and withal of a beautiful countenance and goodly to
look to." This would render him the more acceptable to the people. Even in this qualification, he
was equal to his brother Eliab, who had been rejected by the Lord, and in the qualities of the
heart, which the Lord valued above all else, David
was by far the superior. The Scripture does not
sanction this popular notion, for some of the most
eminent men of the Bible were subject to infirmities.

Absalom, too, must set the people to talking—
not in criticism, for, doubtless, there was enough
of that already, but in admiration. He assumes a
dignity and magnificence more than royal. The
style of David's living appears to have been plain
and unpretending. He had vast treasures, but
had good use for them in making large donations
to the tabernacle services, and to the temple which
he proposed to have built after his death. Love
of pomp and display was not one of his failings.
The king's plain equipage, no doubt, seemed paltry
and unimposing in the eyes of an Oriental people.
But Absalom proposes to supply what David lacked.
He sets up a splendid equipage. To multiply
horses was in imitation of the heathen, and con-
trary to the divine command. But a divine command is little in the way of Absalom. He knows

that it is a new, and therefore a striking luxury in Israel, and he gets him chariots and horses. He rides proudly along the streets. Fifty footmen run as the guard of his precious body. He creates a profound sensation wherever he goes, or is heard of, and the talk increases. His design is to assert his rank as the heir-apparent. He wishes to illustrate his style of kingliness. What wonder, if the people are dazzled by his grandeur, and say as they stand gazing, That is the proper state and bearing of a king! Had we such a monarch, we might rival Egypt and Assyria!

"The generous David," writes Bishop Hall, "suspects no danger from this studied ostentation. His partial love considers all this splendour as expressive of joy and thankfulness; as designed to do honour to their reconciliation; as well becoming the age, the rank, the beauty, the virtues of Absalom."

But this is not enough. Absalom must talk to the people. He must have their ears, before he can get their hearts. Plutarch tells us, that "Menestheus is said to be the first of mankind, that undertook to be a demagogue, and by his eloquence to ingratiate himself with the people." Granting that he was, it does not deprive Absalom of any eminence in this particular. He is no imitator of Athenian politicians. His acts are original with him. And in sacred history, he appears as "the first to play that very common game

of modern king-craft—assuming the demagogue
for the sake of the despot—willing to be the people's man in order to be the people's master."
Nowhere does the Bible give us a more finished
example of the busy, artful, intriguing, and unscrupulous politician.   He can "smile and smile,
and be a villain."   None bows with more elegance,
none shakes hands with tighter, lingering grasp,
and yet in secret he may laugh at the people as
fools easily caught by flatteries, and say to himself,

> I stole all courtesy from heaven,
> And dressed myself in such humility,
> That I did pluck allegiance from men's hearts,
> Loud shouts and salutations from their mouths,
> Even in the presence of the crowned king.

He brings a singular amount of energy and per-
severance to bear upon his scheme.   He "rises up
early," after a night of, perhaps, restless plotting,
and stands by the way of the gate, to make himself agreeable and useful to all who may be in difficulty.   A great deal of sapping and mining must
be done, and to have it well done, he must do it
himself.   He assumes to be the advocate of popular rights ; the fast and loving friend of the people.

> And now forsooth, takes on him to reform
> Some certain edicts and more strait decrees
> That lie too heavy on the commonwealth ;
> Cries out upon abuses, seems to weep
> Over his country's wrongs ; and by his face,
> The seeming brow of justice, did he win
> The hearts of all that he did angle for.

Many have controversies, petitions and appeals

to lay before the king. Difficulties growing up between the tribes of Israel; losses incurred by the
dwellers on the borders, who have often suffered
from the raids of their heathen neighbours; dama-
ges and back-pay due to those who had suffered or
served in war; contentions between rival chieftains
about their degrees of rank, and urgent requests
for promotion and office, may be daily requiring
the attention of the royal mind. He is overbur-
dened with them. He cannot, in a day, settle the
affairs urgently brought forward. Some must delay, have patience, come again, and not even then
be sure of a hearing. Absalom watches such suit-
ors, and calls out to them, draws them aside, asks
their city and their tribes, inquires into their cause
or complaint, and of course takes the side of every
man who comes. "See, thy matters are good and
right."

But he does not offer to be the advocate of those
who need one to speak for them; nor go to the
king and urge him to attend to the suit. He will
not help his father in this pressure of business and
care, but he throws out an insinuation against him,
to excite a bad opinion of the present administration. "There is no man deputed of the king to
hear thee." None from the king downward will
see that justice is done to the people! Thus

—————He, the nearest to the king,
Lay couchant with his eyes upon the throne,
Ready to spring, waiting a chance; for this,

11 *

He chilled the popular praises of the king
With silent smiles of low disparagement.

And then, in his pretended pity for them, and his great desire to relieve them of the injuries they suffer from the neglect of the court, or the long postponement of their causes, he exclaims, " O that I were made judge in the land, that every man which hath any suit or cause might come unto me, and I would. do him justice !" It would be too daring to wish himself king. And to show what sort of a judge he proposes to be, he meets every man who bows to him, puts forth his hand, and kisses him. " He croucheth and humbleth himself to draw them into his net." They do not see that " such popular humility is treason." They are ready to say, " Oh, that we were judged by such a man as Absalom !" They return home to their tribes, and spread through the country the most glowing accounts of the prince's beauty, his splendid horses, his gilded chariots, his swift out-runners, his devotion to the people's rights, his early rising, his late diligence, his sympathies with the poor and the oppressed, and his amazing condescension. They blaze abroad the abilities which he possesses, and the advantages that may be expected from his reign. Thus " The hearts of the men of Israel are after Absalom." He has not simply won them—he has stolen them. It is a theft. He has no right to them. He has used the most dishonest means to get them. He has played

the hypocrite, and sat as a dissembler. He is a
thief, robbing his father of the people's love, patriotism, loyalty, and willing obedience. They com-
plain of the administration. They grumble at the
lawful tithes and taxes. They are slow to support the government. All seems to go wrong, and
nothing will be right until Absalom reigns.

David does not yet perceive the vast robbery.
He is the rather glad to see his brilliant son rising
in the popular favour. Perhaps he has commended
Absalom for his winning manners and his interest
in the people. It is said that Philip of Macedon
wrote to his son Alexander, advising him to draw
to himself the minds of the people by a generous
style of speech and a winning address. It may
have been thus with David. He will not discover
this bold robbery until he is driven from the throne
—nay, not until after Absalom has perished, and
he endeavours to unite the people again in allegiance to himself. Then he will find a strife of parties, a revolt of the ten tribes, and the seditious
cry raised aloud, "We have no part in David, neither have we inheritance in the son of Jesse; every
man to his tents, O Israel!" Then he will know
how extensive the mischief of the princely robber,
when under his father's protection, he "stole the
hearts of the men of Israel."

Well has it been written, "He that trifles with
the affections, or steals the heart of another, for his
own pleasure, or interest, is equally unprincipled,"

as he who robs a bank, or plunders his neighbour's goods.   In God's sight, it may be a greater crime. " He that seduces a young person from his duty and regard to his parents ; he that lures a young inquirer from the Christian minister or friend who is guiding him ; above all, he that tries to withdraw one from his duty to God, and from the love of Christ, on pretence of making him happier elsewhere, is not only guilty of stealing, but is committing his daring theft on the most hallowed ground and on the falsest pretences.   Let the young and inexperienced beware of those who attempt to steal away their hearts from their parents, their teachers, their ministers, their more grave and serious friends."

> Let not the serpent tongue,
> Prompt to deceive, with adulation smooth,
> Gain on your purposed will.

CHAPTER X.

All Israel in Rebellion.

He was a man
Who stole the livery of the court of heaven,
To serve the devil in.—POLLOK.

THE plot of Absalom was now ripe for execution. The date given is, "After forty years." Forty years after what? The return of the prince from exile? This could not be, for David reigned only thirty-three years in Jerusalem. It was, probably, but four years after his return, as stated by Josephus. Some have supposed that the reading should be four, instead of forty. Or was it forty years after David took the throne? This would make the rebellion occur in the last year of his reign, which is not probable. The date may be reckoned from the time when David was anointed by Samuel; or from the time that the people first desired a king, and therefore, in the fortieth year of the monarchy. Matthew Henry adopts this last view, and says; "It is fitly dated from thence, to show that the same restless spirit was still working, and still they were given to change; as fond now of a

new man, as then of a new model." It may be
put down as occurring in about the thirtieth year
of David's reign, when Absalom was about twenty-
five years old.

The moment chosen by Absalom to strike the
blow, was doubtless the most favourable that he
could find.   No war called his father into the field,
so that he could stir up a war behind him and seize
the throne.   This fact, however, most likely, had
an effect upon the army which Absalom noticed
with pleasure.   The rank and file of the army were
not kept up.   Long furloughs may have been
granted to the soldiers, and they engaged at their
homes.   Disorganization had begun.   Military
discipline was relaxed.   The men in service may
have been sent here and there, to guard the borders.   No large body of forces was near the capital.   Only a few trusty bands were ready to serve
the king at an hour's warning.   Joab seemed to be
reposing, and had it not been for the affair of burning the general's barley, Absalom might dare to
approach him with his plot.   Thus the king was
off his guard, and unprepared for a great outbreak.
If in sudden alarm he should call for men, they
would not come, for the prince had stolen their
hearts.

But this does not seem to be all.   A great
change has come over the king.   He is not the
warrior that he once was.   He has hung up his
armour and sheathed his sword as if resolved to

fight no more. He seems humbled and broken-
hearted; his spirit reviving mostly when his voice
chimes with his harp in a new song, or when he
talks of the plans for the temple. And still further: he seems to be disabled and infirm. There are
allusions in the Psalms to an almost fatal illness, and
to treachery practised upon him during that illness.
"I am feeble and sore broken. . . . . They also
that seek after my life lay snares for me." (Ps.
xxxviii., xxxix.) At such a time Absalom might
find some small pretext for uttering a fling at the
administration, and the inefficiency of his father in
judging the causes of the people. Some have supposed, that soon after this long illness Absalom
brought his rebellion to a crisis. It gives us a yet
darker impression of his villainy and hardness of
heart, if he chose a time when his father was just
recovering from disease, to inflict upon his aged
head a crowning sorrow and disgrace, if not indeed
a deadly blow.

The place of rendezvous was wisely chosen.
Everything favoured Hebron. It was so near Jerusalem that a night's hasty march would make the
distance. It had been the seat of government, and
the birth-place of the prince, which would give
some advantage to his pretensions. It is possible
that the removal of the throne from that ancient
and sacred city was a wound upon the inhabitants
which time had not healed. They, perhaps, felt
deprived of their rights, and cherished a lingering

discontent, in which nearly all Judah would naturally participate. Absalom may have counted upon their dissatisfaction. Moreover, the people had once been ready to hail and support David when he appeared to be in revolt against Saul, and why not as quickly welcome and aid Absalom against David? Hebron was, also, a stronghold easily defended. The rebels could post themselves among the windings of the mountains, and bar out all attacking forces.

There was something, not only in the position, but in the spirit of Judah to encourage Absalom, more than in any other tribe. From the first it had been disposed to claim pre-eminence, and to act for itself. Each tribe had its own local government and its ruler, (1 Chron. xxvii. 16–22), and sometimes the doctrine of tribe-rights, or "state rights," was advocated, but it was speedily rebuked and its tendency checked. But the rights of Judah were not simply those of a tribe; they were those of a great party. Already had Judah, embracing Benjamin, been upon one side, and the ten tribes on the other. Absalom could more easily gain the one tribe of Judah, and its strong party, than the ten tribes, if he should not be able to gain the entire twelve.

Yet he hoped, and prepared to secure them all. His grand robbery, in stealing the hearts of the people, gave him confidence enough to order them to raise the standard of revolt in every tribe. He sent spies far and wide, to be ready for the signal trump, and then proclaim aloud, "Absalom reigneth in Hebron."

And now what does he propose as a motive for going to Hebron? A feast? That might call up Baal-hazor and awaken suspicion. A princely excursion? That might secure him too much uninvited company. A visit to his birth-place? That would not afford him company enough of the sort he wished. But a vow—a holy pilgrimage—nothing could be better, for a cloak of religion will cover his treachery. A lie will serve his purpose, for nobody can disprove his declaration. It will completely deceive his father, though it be a solemn mockery of God. It is difficult to sound the depth of villainy and hypocrisy which could frame the plea made to his father, with such apparent deference and submission. "I pray thee, let me go and pay my vow, which I have vowed unto the Lord [to be redeemed] in Hebron. For thy servant vowed a vow while I abode at Geshur in Syria, saying, If the Lord shall bring me again indeed to Jerusalem, then I will serve the Lord." In this there was falsehood somewhere. If he had never made such a vow, then he invented a lie. If he had made such a vow, then he knew that he was false in saying, "I will serve the Lord." Such a real sincere service never came within the scope of his honest intentions. "Seeming devotion doth but gild the knave."

12

David is easily deceived.   He knows how often
men make vows in their times of trouble.   Jacob,
in his anxiety and fear, "vowed a vow, saying, If
God will be with me, and will keep me in this way
that I go, and will give me bread to eat, and rai-
ment to put on, so that I come again to my father's
house in peace; then shall the Lord be my God."
May not David believe that his son imitated so excellent an example? and the king knows how to
fulfil them, saying, "I will go into thy house with
burnt-offerings; I will pay thee my vows, which
my lips have uttered, and my mouth hath spoken
when I was in trouble."   How ready then is he to
believe all the good he can of his son, and to think
that he is now about to imitate the better conduct
of his father!   "How glad is the good old king,
that he is blessed with so pious a son!"   It is well
that the very letter of so holy a vow be fulfilled!
Let him go to Hebron. The words, "Go in peace,"
indicate a father's blessing upon him.   In the
world there have been vile characters enough, but
even hypocrisy can furnish very few with blacker
hearts than that of Absalom.   How good the religion which men thus counterfeit!   Every act of
religious hypocrisy is a commendation of the real
value of true religion.   Yet "hypocritical piety is
but double iniquity."

Absalom was very choice of his company for this
pilgrimage.   He would not have in his train only
"lewd fellows of the baser sort," however conge-

nial to him. He culled out two hundred men, no
doubt sober, substantial citizens, and invited them
to attend the feast upon his sacrifice. They went
in their simplicity of heart, and knew not anything
of the deep treachery underlying his pretensions.
He dare not trust them with his plot, for they were
loyal men, who would shrink in abhorrence from a
design upon the throne. But their presence would
lead the common people to suppose that they had
deserted the king, and were supporting the prince.
If David's best friends had forsaken him, why
should anybody pretend to regard loyalty as too
sacred to be renounced?

At Hebron, Absalom ventured upon the solemn
rites of sacrifice. How this would give him favour
with the inhabitants, and peaceable possession of
the city! It would provide him a feast, they fur-
nishing the provisions. So devout a prince would
find them in eager rivalry to show him hospitality.
What thanksgivings he must have offered for his
safe return from Geshur! But he fears to rely altogether upon his own craftiness. He wants advice. The pirate ship may wreck in getting it out
to sea, unless he have a skilful pilot.

He has already learned the right man for the
helm, and sends for him. And now appears a conspirator who was the equal of Absalom in baseness
—Ahithophel, a crafty but most able man, once
high in the councils of David, and whose capacity
largely consisted in a total lack of conscience. He

was now acting in the import of his name, and was literally the "brother of foolishness;" a very singular name for one who was renowned, throughout all Israel, for his political sagacity. Absalom had stolen his heart, a thing not hard to do, for it was open to the plunder of his allegiance. For some reason he had left the court, and was at Giloh his native town. Perhaps, either king or counsellor has become disgusted with the other, and this familiar friend, in whom David trusted, which did eat of his bread, as Judas, afterwards, did that of his Lord, was ready to enter into a conspiracy. Absalom knew the importance of such a man to his cause, for "the counsel of Ahithophel, which he counselled in those days, was as if a man had inquired at the oracle of God." The people had so regarded it with David, and would be ready to give it the same weight if thrown on the side of Absalom.

The prince seems now to be king. His movement has prospered to a wish. Cheering news come in from every quarter. The strategies have been complete. The trumpet has rolled the signal through the land. At place after place, the proclamation has been made, and the people have declared for Absalom. Some are ready to believe that the king is dying, or dead. Some are restless for a new ruler. Some remember how they were advised and caressed by the condescending prince. Some do not quite like the movement, but think that it will succeed at any rate, and they may as well worship success. Many fear a dreadful war, when prices must rise, taxes increase, property be destroyed, and brothers meet each other on fields of slaughter, and they imagine that the shortest method of staying these horrors is to let the rebellion have its way. Patriotism yields to policy. Others shout for the usurper, rejoicing in the very ungodliness that has made effective his appeal to the hearts of the people. And thus it goes on increasing in every city and hamlet, until the conspiracy is strong. The uprising is so general that those who are half in fear, and half in favour, scarcely call it a rebellion. It is a revolution in their eyes. It is a great protest against the administration; or by some softer name they aid the treason. The people flock to the standard of revolt in such numbers that the whole nation seems to be giving its adherence to Absalom. Soldiers come, and there is no scarcity, of course, in the voluntary supplies of officers. All the men of Israel seem to be upon the ground. An army begins to be organized, such as never had been marshalled in the vale of Hebron. In their enthusiasm they grow wild in their wickedness. They seem to ridicule the piety, as well as the power of David, and boast that even God cannot help or deliver him. In the second Psalm David refers to the vast multitudes gathering to the prince's standard, as "Ten thousands of people." And he prays in calmness of spirit,

12 *

"Lord, how are they increased that trouble me? How many are they that rise up against me! Many there be which say of my soul, There is no help for him in God."

We may suppose that there came to Absalom many of those classes of people, who once enlisted under David when he hid in the cave of Adullam, and needed an army against Saul. "And every one that was in distress, and every one that was in debt, and every one that was discontented, gathered themselves unto him." Poor material for an army, one would suppose, so far as the moral element was concerned, but the best that David once could get, and now the very sort that well suits Absalom. David could reform such men, but there is no hope of their improvement under the prince, unless they are moved by a disgust of his impiety to aim at the extreme from his example. With his troop of noble men whom he has deceived, of bad men whom he has attracted, of soldiers and office-seekers, of hangers-on and stragglers and desperados, the prince prepares to march towards Jerusalem.

He has all the encouragement that outward success can impart. But does not conscience rebuke and check him? He must need to make repeated effort to silence it. He must sometimes stand astonished and aghast, when he thinks of what he is about to do. Amid all the excitement of successful schemes a vague horror must steal upon his soul. A dark vision of outraged justice must haunt him. He may scare away the hideous spectre, but he cannot lay it in its grave. And he surrenders himself to his vile counsellor Ahithophel, as Judas lent himself to Satan.

CHAPTER XI.

The Flight of the King.

He who hath never warred with misery,
Nor ever tugged with fortune and distress
Hath had no occasion, nor no field to try
The strength and forces of his worthiness.
For only men show their abilities,
And what they arc in their extremities.

"And there came a messenger to David, saying,
The hearts of the men of Israel are after Absalom."
The king can surmise the rest. The plot, the
heart-stealing, the vow, the visit to Hebron, are all
revealed in a flash; a moment more and the thunders of war may be heard. Yet not a word of astonishment or a wail of helplessness is heard from
his lips. Nor is he stunned into silence, and stu-
pified by fear. He speaks as one who sees the
wisest course to take, in the same flash that has
disclosed the overhanging danger.

David is always great in adversity. In the fur-
nace glows the gold. His greatness does not depend on his royalty. It is within his lofty soul,
and is inseparable from his commanding character.

And now when many other men would be distracted
or shocked, neither his piety, nor his generosity,
nor his prudence desert him. His goodness, patience, and resignation are much as ever conspicuous. He is now self-possessed, though in haste.
It is no time for deliberation. Yet in his speedy
action there is no flutter nor bewilderment. In
his conduct you see the training of the veteran
warrior who has often had to act in sudden emer-
gencies and perilous surprises. We think, at
once, of our own great Washington, in the darkest
hour of the revolution, when the enemy was pressing in with forces too strong to resist; when his
wise and quick retreats began to be called disgraces
by those who had more envy than valour in their
souls; when his friends grew fewer in numbers and
fainter in heart; when his jealous .rivals were suspected of conspiring against him from motives quite
as base as those of Absalom or Arnold; when patriots were faltering, and a brave army was almost
worn down into despair; and when, with feelings
something like those of David at the outburst of
the rebellion against the throne and liberties of
Israel, he wrote to congress, "You can form no
idea of the perplexity of my situation. No man, I
believe, ever had a greater choice of evils, and less
means to extricate himself from them. However,
under a full persuasion of the justice of our cause,
I cannot entertain an idea that it will finally sink,
though it may remain for some time under a cloud."

There he was, like both David and St. Paul, "troubled on every side, yet not distressed; perplexed, but not in despair; persecuted, but not forsaken; cast down, but not destroyed." How great in adversity! It was the element in which his highest graces shone out. Then his quick eye saw at a glance, the bold measures for the sudden emergency, saying, in reference to what seemed an assumption of power, "A character to lose, an estate to forfeit, the inestimable blessings of liberty at stake, and a life devoted, must be my excuse." Sublime spirit! whose fatherly love for his country Heaven knew better than the people whom he served, and breathing kindly upon the gloom God dispersed it, and standing on the banks of the Delaware, he said, "Go over," and making Trenton the door of hope, he turned victory to our armies, and to our land deliverance. Transfer this power to act wisely and promptly in extremities of need to the king of Israel, and learn how

> Affliction is the good man's shining scene;
> Prosperity conceals his brightest ray;
> As night to stars, woe lustre gives to man.

Great generals are known by their wise retreats, as well as by their successful engagements, provided that they seize upon every promising opportunity for victory. King David sees at once, that he must retreat from Jerusalem. He is not surprised into cowardice. King James II. of England, when he knew that William of Orange was hastening with an army against London, took fright, thought of himself, feared his personal fate, and secretly escaped from the capital, leaving the people as unprotected sheep to the mercies of the incoming shepherd. It was well that he did; the coming prince was not a wolf. But David was not an hireling, fleeing, and leaving the flock to the wolf Absalom. Not himself alone, but the people, must be saved from violence. His retreat was dictated by motives of policy and humanity.

Safety demanded it. In saving himself he was saving the crown. The authority to govern would still be vested in him. He could leave the city and yet not surrender the throne. "Arise, and let us flee, for we shall not else escape from Absalom; make speed to depart lest he overtake us suddenly and bring evil upon us."

Another reason for leaving Jerusalem was, lest Absalom should "smite the city with the edge of the sword." In his humanity, David was anxious to ward off the contest, and save the crowded capital from murder and rapine. It were better to carry the war into the wilderness, where property would not be exposed, and the lives of innocent women and children endangered. His heart was set upon Jerusalem, and he could not bear the thought of her walls being stormed, her towers razed, her palaces laid in the dust. Let the blow fall upon him, and not the city which he preferred

above his chief joy. Here were patriotism and
piety ; a love for country overruling all personal
considerations, and a devotion to the church which
made personal sacrifices little in his own eyes ; what
matter if the commander risk, or even lose his life,
so that the ship and all her precious freight be
saved!

It did not seem possible to defend the city
against the rebels. The monthly quota of the
militia was not present, owing to the disorganization of the army that had begun to prevail. In
the time of peace, he had not kept himself prepared
for war. And where was Joab, the general-in-
chief? He does not appear upon the scene. He
ought to have had his eye upon the movements of
the conspirators. What wonder if the king more
than half suspected that his ingenuities and persistence in restoring Absalom, were a part of the rebellious scheme. Or was he hesitating, and weigh-
ing the matter in the balance, to see which party
would have the decisive power, the government
and the dispensation of offices ? Strange that he
has not appeared already, urging the king to take
speedy measures for suppressing the forming rebellion. But wait, he will yet come forth, loyal to
his king, and in fury against the arch-rebel on the
field. David had some reason to believe that the
arts of the prince had so corrupted the people in
the very capital that the city was full of spies, in-
triguers, informers, and desperate traitors. There

might be rebels in his own cabinet, and his own house. Only his "servants"—his reliable and honourable friends ever ready to serve him—seemed to be with him when the alarming report came to his ears. He had reason to fear that he was

> Deserted at his utmost need,
> By those his former bounty fed.

And all Israel might be in defection and rebellion. If strong and loyal Judah was open to Absalom; if Hebron was in the rebel's hands; if none of Benjamin's almost sixty thousand warriors were upon the ground; if none of the veterans who had marched and triumphed with him in his earlier campaigns were present in the enthusiasm of their loyalty; if none of the victors who had conquered Philistia, smitten Moab, broken the Northern League, humbled the southern powers of Edom, and demolished Rabbath-Ammon, were gathering to his defence, and if it seemed vain to call for men, and ruinous to wait for their coming, how could he hope to defend the city against the insurgents, who had prepared themselves for the onset and might at any hour come storming through the defenceless gates? He fears that,

> ——— the hearts
> Of all his people shall revolt from him,
> And kiss the lips of unacquainted change.

Not yet does he know that a few tried bands are faithful. Not until he has packed for the depar-

13

ture, and left all in order at his palace, and gone
forth to a place afar off, lingering to see that all
his servants and family are safe as they pass on
beside him, does he seem to know that a few soldiers are loyal and ready to cast in their fortune
with that of the king. The Cherethites and Pe-
lethites are there in their full numbers, under their
bold captain, Benaiah, one of David's three
mighties, and afraid of neither lions, Moabites, nor
Egyptians.* There, too, in the train, are the Git-
tites, six hundred men which came after him from
Gath, once Philistines, but now devoted friends,
and with the others composing the body guard of
the king, the "legion of honour," or the royal
brigade. While Absalom is acting worse than an
alien, these foreigners are exhibiting the spirit of
adopted sons. When foreigners are so ready to
sustain an administration, it is a good proof of the
mildness and justice of the government.

And now we have one of the most touching
scenes and affecting specimens of an unselfish
king and a loyal subject. David would force no
man to remain in his service, especially if he must
share the perils in prospect. "Good men, when
they suffer themselves, care not how few are involved with them in suffering. Generous souls are
more concerned at the shares others have in their
troubles, than at their own." The king's eye falls
upon Ittai the Gittite, who had, probably been a

* 2 Sam. viii. 18; xxiii. 20-23.

leading man among the Philistines, had lately left
his country, sought adoption in the kingdom and
city of David, and considered himself a naturalized
citizen. There was no moral obligation upon him
to volunteer his services, and no sordid motive in
his heart in continuing as the captain of the Git-
tites. A stranger and an exile he was not bound
to share the trials of a fugitive king, and David
says to him, "Wherefore goest thou also with us?
return to thy place and abide with the [new] king,
for thou art a stranger and also an exile. Whereas
thou comest but yesterday, should I this day make
thee go up and down with us? Seeing I go whither
I may, return thou, and take back thy brethren;
and mercy and truth be with thee."

It has been suggested that David wished thus to
test the loyalty and sincerity of this noble foreigner, by showing him the hardness of the service and the uncertainty of the result. Somewhat
as our Saviour tested the motives and the doctrine
of one who said, "Lord, I will follow thee whither-
soever thou goest," by answering, "Foxes have
holes and birds of the air have nests, but the Son
of man hath not where to lay his head." No
doubt David acted with that noble consideration
for others which so strongly marks his character,
and placed his own interest out of view, but even
on the ground that he wished to bring this captain's
loyalty to the test, we should not lose the force of
his reply. It shows us the true spirit of devotion

to the rightful authority in government, and to the cause of the great Master.   In neither, should the hardness of the service be a reason for declining and going back, and submitting to an authority raised over us by rebellion.   Mere policy and ease are not the decisive considerations.   The principle of right should decide us.   It is right to serve David, and wrong to serve Absalom, and therefore Ittai will go with the lawful king, no matter if he knows not whither he may be driven or what he must endure. He loves his adopted country, and will not desert its constitutional government in a trying hour. Policy is nothing; patriotism rises as far above it as the star of David's night is high above the trembling lamp in the tent of Absalom.   It is a patriotism that will cost him something; even blood may flow for it, and life may be the price thereof.   But it cannot be bartered for the mere exemption from trial and endurance.   It cannot be bought from him by the temptations of Jerusalem. It is a sort of a national wisdom that cannot be gotten from him for gold, neither shall silver be weighed for the price thereof.   It cannot be valued with the gold of Ophir, with the precious onyx or the sapphire.   The exchange of it shall not be made for jewels of fine gold.   And as a noble pa-triot he replies, "As the Lord liveth, and as my lord the king liveth, surely in what place my lord, the king, shall be, whether in death or life, even there also will thy servant be."   It is saying from a heart that loves his country and his king, "Entreat me not to leave thee, or to return from following after thee; for whither thou goest I will go; and where thou lodgest I will lodge; thy people shall be my people, and thy God my God; where thou diest I will die, and there also will I be buried; the Lord do so to me, and more also, if aught but death part thee and me."

And this patriotism is but a type of the piety and devotion which we should cherish towards David's greater Son, the great King in Zion. We should follow him with all this ardour, remembering, "No man having put his hand to the plough and looking back, is fit for the kingdom of God." Through evil and through good report, we should cleave to him, determined that neither life nor death, principalities nor powers, shall separate us from his service and his love. And if in some testing moment, when he seems to be almost deserted, he ask us, "Will ye also go away?" let us be able to reply, "Lord, to whom shall we go but unto thee? Thou hast the words of eternal life."

> To thee we still would cleave
> With ever-growing zeal,
> If millions tempt us Christ to leave,
> Oh let them ne'er prevail.

And our great King will accept our service, as cheerfully as David accepted that of the patriotic foreigner, who gladdened the heart that was beating more in anxiety for his friends than in fear of

13 *

his foes. Nor is this all the encouragement that
David has. The people have not all forsaken and
betrayed him. He does not feel so deserted as our
Lord felt, when on nearly the same path He crossed
the brook Kedron and entered Gethsemane. The
people show their attachment by their tears. "All
the country wept with a loud voice." And, as
Matthew Henry says, "Cause enough there was
for weeping. To see a prince thus reduced; one
that had lived so great, forced from his palace, and
in fear of his life, with a small retinue, seeking
shelter in a desert; the city of David which he
himself won, built, and fortified, made an unsafe
abode for David himself; it would move the compassion even of strangers to see a man fallen thus
low from such a height, and this by the wickedness
of his own son; a piteous case it was. To see him
in this distress, and themselves unable to help him,
might well draw floods of tears from their eyes."
And without sacrilege, he might have turned and
said, as our Lord afterwards did to the daughters
of Jerusalem, as they followed him to Calvary,
"Weep not for me, but for yourselves and your
children."

Nor was this all the sympathy that David received. Added to those who would fight for him,
and weep for him, were those who would pray for
him, and support him by all the consolations of religion. He was surprised to find that in their zeal
for his cause, the priests and Levites had brought

the "ark of the covenant of God" from the city,
and proposed that it should be borne with the king.
It was the symbol of God's presence.   They
thought that the interests of the government and
the interests of the church were closely allied, and
should not be separated.   The ark should go with
its protector, that God may the more surely pro-
tect him.   Once "David would not rest until he
had found a resting-place for the ark ; and now if
the priests may have their mind, the ark shall not
rest until David returns to his rest."   Its presence
would afford him great advantage.   It would in-
vest his cause with sacredness in the eyes of all
good men.   They would hope the more strongly,
that God's favour would be secured to him.   Its
absence from Absalom would also suggest the absence of God's countenance, and help to prove the
utter ungodliness of his rebellion.   But the king
objected to this movement.   God had said of Zion,
"This is my rest, here will I dwell," and even under this unexpected emergency, David would not
disturb that arrangement.   The hurry of flight
and the tumult of battle did not befit that sacred
symbol.   God's presence was not limited to the
ark, nor would its return exclude religion from the
army.   He sent it back, and the priests also, car-
ing more for the church's prosperity than for his
own welfare, and saying with hope for the best,
and resignation to the worst, "If I shall find favour in the eyes of the Lord, he will bring me

again, and show me both it, and his habitation. But if he thus say, I have no delight in thee ; behold here I am, let him do to me as seemeth good unto him.''

The priests were to watch events in the city, and send word to the king of what was transpiring. Thus he would learn wisdom from the rebels, from the ministers of God, and from a superintending Providence. If the priests were not to fight, they were, at least, to lend their loyal aid to the government when he was attacked by those who sought to usurp it. With such wise arrangements behind him, he directed his way to "the plain of the wilderness'' toward Jericho.

"He intended," writes Dr. Kitto, "to proceed to the country beyond the Jordan, and then collect his resources and watch the progress of events. From the people beyond the river he had received many proofs of attachment, and his wars had brought him much into connection with them, and had materially advanced their prosperity, and he thought that he might count on their fidelity. The geographical position was also well suited to his purpose, and the step seems to have been, under all the circumstances, the best that could have been taken.''

CHAPTER XII.

David Wept.

Woe awaits a country when
She sees the tears of bearded men.

It is the second time that David's tears over Absalom's criminal conduct have been impressed upon the Scripture page. Under the excitement of arranging his escape from the city, getting the troops, the people and "the little ones" over the brook Kedron, and planning the future march, he could perhaps refrain from tears. The multitude wept for him, but he must bear up with more than manly strength, or their wild commotion would hinder the flight. But as soon as the stress of thought is over, and the mind relaxes, his feelings overpower him. He realizes his situation. He cannot forget Jerusalem, and for her his tears must fall. In such haste has he escaped, that he is not only on foot, but bare-foot. For shame and in mortification he covers his head. We may imagine him going forth as an old man, a miserable fugitive, driven forth from a people whose independence as a nation he has established, and by the cruelties of a son whose life has been his gift : and as he looks back, from the first hill that he climbs, upon the city once captured by his arms, built up by his toils, beautified by his enterprise, and made glorious by the presence of the Lord's tabernacle which he brought into it with rejoicing, he gives way to the anguish caused by the memories of the past, the dangers of the present, and the darkness of the future. No scowl is on his brow, no scorn upon his lips, no murmur—nothing but a great out-gushing grief. But no imaginary picture can be so striking as that drawn by inspiration, for God traced the outlines, and He excels all others in portraying the grief of his servants. "And David went up by the ascent of Mount Olivet, and wept as he went up, and had his head covered, and he went barefoot; and all the people that was with him, covered every man his head, and they went up, weeping as they went up."

King David in his offices and character was a type of our Lord Jesus Christ—imperfect type, but the best that humanity could furnish. It was de-signed that he should throw a strong light upon the person, character, offices, work and sufferings of the great Redeemer. We can understand the hu-man, and this may lead us to the Divine. David's oneness with his people, ever identifying himself with them in joy and sorrow, is a type of the one-ness of Christ and all believers. In David's ma-jesty and mildness as a king, we see the figure of

Him who is the Lion and the Lamb. David's loyalty to God earned him the title, "My servant
David;" thus fore-shadowing the devotedness of
him to whom the Father declared, "This is my beloved Son, in whom I am well pleased." The
ancient saints based their idea of the coming Messiah very much upon the character of David. And
hence when Jesus came with wondrous works, and
words more wondrous still, "The people were
amazed and said, Is not this the Son of David?"
It was the popular title given him. By that name
the people praised him, and the afflicted begged for
mercy. It had come to be the common sentiment,
that to the warm, fatherly heart of Israel's greatest king, no appeal for compassion was ever made
in vain, and thus the unfortunate and the sinful
came to think that in Jesus they might have "The
sure mercies of David."

But in David's *sorrowful experiences* he comes
nearest to the man of sorrows. His hard discipline
was a type of Christ's baptism of suffering. Alike
they were betrayed, one by his own son, the other
by his own disciple. Alike they endured the most
painful trials as the result of treachery; one being
driven out of the gates of Jerusalem by fear of the
insurgents; the other by the force of the people,
he bearing his own cross. Alike they were forsaken; one by his favourite tribe of Judah, which
first chose him as their king, and of which he had
a right to expect an unswerving loyalty; the other

by some of his most favoured disciples who were among the first to follow him, and the most forward to profess their undying attachment. Alike they found some of their best friends in need to be almost strangers. One supported by such men as Ittai the exile, Shobi of desolate Rabbah, and the old, blind Barzillai, who was an embodiment of the modern Christian commission; the other pitied even by the compromising Pilate, embalmed by Nicodemus, and entombed by the kindness of Joseph of Arimathea. In both cases a period of accumulated agonies was succeeded by glimpses of the Divine favour, and the assurance of final deliverance; each drank of the brook of heavenly refreshment by the way, until at length, God lifted up the head, and lightened the heart. But especially in one sorrow do they meet. David wept. Jesus wept.

Though centuries apart, they stood on the same ground—Olivet. They overlooked the same city —Jerusalem. On the same road, (it would seem) they met. One going from the city with a sorrowful multitude; the other coming in with a rejoicing crowd. One leaving a throne for a time because a rebellious son was usurping it; the other having left his throne of glory to bring a rebellious province back to its allegiance unto God. And in many respects the cause of their tears was the same. Each bore a burden of sin. One pressed down by his own sins; the other by the sins of us all, for he bare our iniquities.

No doubt there was an element of self-conviction in David's tears. For a long time—ever since he worded the fifty-first Psalm—he has felt the sting of his own sin. It has lain heavy upon him. It has taken away his health, and in an ungodly man it would have become remorse and despair. Tears have been his drink day and night. He has felt reproach, for he has caused the enemies of the Lord to blaspheme. He is a greatly changed man, going down to his grave mourning. His piety is not so buoyant, exultant, triumphant; it is repressed, humble, suffering, patient. "Alas for him! The bird which once rose to heights unattained before by mortal wing filling the air with its joyful songs, now lies with maimed wing upon the ground, pouring forth its doleful cries unto God."

Though his sins have been pardoned, yet some of their temporal results are pressing upon him. If not his sin now, because he has cast the entire awful burden on the Lord, it is found again in the sins of Absalom and his fellow conspirators, and these burden his soul. He takes them upon himself, not because he can atone for them, but because, in some degree, his conduct has caused them. The very wind from Jerusalem seems to bring them to Olivet and lay their weight upon him until he weeps. "He never wept thus when Saul hunted him, but a wounded conscience makes trouble lie heavy." With all caution, let us draw a

14

lesson from the mysterious resemblance between
David and Christ, remembering, as we mark the
agony which the sense of sin gave to David, that a
far greater agony was impressed on the soul of
Jesus by the sins of his people. Never had they
been his by nature or by commission; never had
he caused them, but they were taken up by him
that he might make for them a complete atonement.
Under the imputed burden he weeps on Olivet.

David weeps over one sinner, and he a son. It
was an overwhelming grief at the desperate wickedness of one whom he most dearly loved. "If it
had been an enemy that had done this, then I could
bear it: if one that hated me thus rose up against
me, then I could hide myself from him. But it is
thou, my son, my son, Absalom! thou my expected
peace, but now thy father's enemy: thou so caressed in thy infancy, kissed after thy crime when
life was forfeited, and indulged in thy princely displays while thou wast stealing all Israel from me;
thou, who hast rebelled against me, plunged the
kingdom into war and anarchy, and braved the
wrath of thy God! O Absalom, my son, my son!"

> Did Christ o'er sinners weep?
> And shall our cheeks be dry?
> Let floods of penitential grief
> Burst forth from every eye.
> The Son of God in tears,
> Angels with wonder see;
> Be thou astonished O, my soul,
> He shed those tears for thee.

And as David thinks of the rising enmity against him, the war that may bring its horrors upon Jerusalem, and the riot that shall prevail upon her streets, may not his tears be like those of our Lord when " He beheld the city and wept over it, saying, If thou hadst known, even thou, at least, in this thy day, the things which belong unto thy peace! but now they are hid from thine eyes?" Even Jerusalem does not know David to be its real king, nor the largeness of his heart in planning for its good! And thinking of his rejection by the people, whom he would gather into the solid and enduring unity of a peaceful, prosperous nation, and into the one church of God, so that all Israel might dwell under the shadow of the Almighty, and under his wings be sheltered from every earthly storm, may not David have emotions like those expressed by our Lord when he said, " O Jerusalem, Jerusalem, which killest the prophets, and stonest them that are sent unto thee; how often would I have gathered thy children together, as a hen doth gather her brood under her wings, and ye would not! Behold your house is left unto you desolate: and verily I say unto you, Ye shall not see me, until the time come when ye shall say, Blessed is he that cometh in the name of the Lord?"

If from the " town of Mansoul" we have expelled the true King of the heart, and given the enemy an entrance and a welcome, let us think of Jesus weeping over it, and then give Him a triumphal

entry, that our sin—not our Saviour—may be crucified in it, and that He may reign, the King of
glory, ever blessing, and blessed for evermore.
Then no tear of Christ shall have dropped, and no
blood of His have been shed for us in vain. Shall
these tears rise up against us? We have seen the
rain-drops fall, when sunshine mingled with the
shower, and heaven was spanned by the bow in the
cloud. All was then gladdening; we had the smiling earth, the weeping skies, and had no dread of
furious storms. But these drops that fell as glis-
tening tears did not waste in the earth's long
thirsty soil. They rose again. The very sun that
shone when they were raining down in mercy,
called them forth, and sent them floating in clouds
for another mission. They gathered thicker, they
drifted about, they hung threatening over us, they
grew darker, blacker, and more fearful, and at last
burst upon us like a storm of judgment, chilling
where they struck, or freezing as they fell. And
shall a Saviour's tears enter as an element in the
destroying storm, that must fall upon sinners on
the great day of the Lord, which hasteth greatly,
as " a day of wrath, a day of trouble and distress,
a day of wasteness and desolation, a day of darkness and gloominess, a day of clouds and thick
darkness," when " the earth shall quake, the heavens shall tremble; the sun and the moon shall be
dark, and the stars shall withdraw their shining;
and the Lord shall utter his voice before his army,

for his camp is very great; for he is strong that executeth his word; for the day of the Lord is great and very terrible; and who can abide it? The great day of his wrath is come, and who shall be able to stand?" Not those who remain unmoved by a Saviour's weeping tenderness, and unredeemed by his atoning blood. Not those who refuse the pities of Christ on Olivet, and his pardon on Calvary. How oft would he have gathered them, and covered them from the approaching storm, but they would not! How oft he visited them, but they knew not the day of their visitation! How oft would he have dwelt in the house of their heart, but now it is left desolate! How oft did he reveal unto them the things that belong to their peace, but they hid them from their eyes! Jesus wept, but they had no tears of penitence. Jesus shed his blood, but they sought no remission of sins. And who shall stand? They who yield to the infinite love that prompted those tears on Olivet. They who have an eternal refuge beneath the almighty wing through which no storm shall beat, and which no tempest of hail shall sweep away. They who have gone to the fountain and have washed their robes white in the blood of the Lamb. These are they who shall " be accounted worthy to escape all these things that shall come to pass, and to stand before the Son of man."

14 *

CHAPTER XIII.

Friends and Foes.

The more the bold, the bustling, and the bad
Press to usurp the reins of power, the more
Behooves it virtue, with indignant zeal
To check their combination.

THE feather of Absalom is found on his associates and on those who are ready to flock to his
standard. We do not yet find a moral man named
among his followers. Nor can we expect it. It
requires a low degree of immorality to engage in
such a conspiracy. The reports of Absalom's revolt had spread far and wide, and evil men seize
upon the moment to conspire against loyal masters
or to curse the Lord's anointed. In them all we
see the treacherous spirit of the prince.

Perhaps David's tears were stayed by astonishment. Some one told him that "Ahithophel was
among the conspirators with Absalom." This gave
him more alarm than anything that had yet occurred, for, as Matthew Henry quaintly says, "One
good head in such a design is worth a thousand
good hands. Absalom was himself no politician,

[statesman, rather, for he was demagogue enough] but he had got one entirely in his interest that was, and would be the more dangerous because he had been, all along, acquainted with David's counsels and affairs; if therefore he could be baffled, Absalom was as good as routed, and the head of the conspiracy cut off." The king prayed earnestly that the counsel of Ahithophel might be turned into foolishness, alluding probably to his name—"brother of foolishness." "He names the person whose counsel he prays against. God gives us leave, in prayer, to be humbly and reverently free with him, and to mention the particular care, fear, and grief that lies heavy upon us. He prays, not against Ahithophel's person, but against his counsel."

On the top of the mount, up which he had wept, he worshipped God, and as if in answer to prayer, there came a man to him wise enough to defeat the advice of the prince's counsellor. Hushai the Archite came to meet his king, "with his coat rent and earth upon his head," in token of the deepest grief. "Unto whom David said, If thou passest on with me, then thou shalt be a burden unto me, but if thou return unto the city, and say unto Absalom, I will be thy servant, O king; as I have been thy father's servant hitherto, so will I now also be thy servant; then mayest thou for me defeat the counsel of Ahithophel." The policy was shrewd and far-seeing, but the principle was not worthy of David. We see no way to defend it. It was proposing a deception, a strategy by fraud. The best that can be made of it is, that David thought the traitor deserved to be betrayed. He went on the principle of fighting Absalom with his own weapons. He would pay the prince in his own coin. If treachery was to be the current coin of Absalom's realm he should have plenty of it.

And when David was a little past the top of the hill, he came in contact with one of the darker specimens of humanity on whom the glare of Absalom's guilt seems to fall. Ziba was the very man to make a speculation out of the rebellion, at the expense of a loyal master. He was one of those men who have a sharp eye upon their own interest, and when any selfish gain appears,

> That moment a mere voice, a straw, a shadow,
> Are capable of turning them aside.

To understand him, we must bring up the touching story of his master Mephibosheth. He was five years old when his father Jonathan was slain. As David had been for, at least, six years a wanderer in the wilderness, hunted by Saul, he knew nothing of this child of his dear friend. When the father and grandfather of Mephibosheth fell on Gilboa, the rumour went abroad, and all of the house of Saul were terrified lest they should be exterminated. The nurse in her fright ran with the child, fell, or let him fall, and thereby he was lamed

for life. The helpless infant was carried beyond
the Jordan, and brought up in the house of the
generous Machir at Lo-debar in Gilead. There he
remained in obscurity until David was well established on the throne, and was inquiring for any of
the house of Saul that remained, that he might
show him a kindness for Jonathan's sake. Ziba,
a servant of that house, was heard of and sent for.
He told that Jonathan had a son, lame in his feet.
David sent for him, quelled his fears, made him a
guest at his table, and restored to him the estate
of Saul. Ziba was the manager of his lands. And
still this lame prince was to be pitied, for neither
mind nor body had fair play. Very likely he had
been often outwitted by his rascally servant.

When David was fleeing from the city, Mephibosheth soon heard of it, and prepared to follow.
He was not lame in his loyalty, and wished to be
with his king. But Ziba interfered, offering to
convey the generous supplies to David. The servant had a base plot to make himself greater than
his master. He offered the noble present of bread,
raisins, and wine to the king, to open the way for
an invented slander. He declared that his master
had remained in Jerusalem, saying, " To-day shall
the house of Israel restore me the kingdom of my
father." The lie seemed plausible. David too
hastily believed the deceiver, confiscated the property of Mephibosheth, and gave it to Ziba. Our
wonder is that this swindler did not go at once to

Absalom, and get the arch rebel to make the gift.
But he was one who thought it best to have "two
strings to his bow," and he must first have David's
grant of the estate.   It is not likely that Ziba expected David to return to the throne, and we are
quite ready to suspect that he now hastened to
fawn for a smile and a gift of the lands from Absalom.

Still farther on the king was hounded by one of
the "angry spirits and turbulent mutterers of
stifled treason," whose valour consists in barking
behind the hedge.   Shimei came forth to curse and
threat rebellion.   He was of the house of Saul, and
doubtless had experienced a great fall in the world,
and this goes far to account for his insolent rage.
He thought that David was for ever down, and Absalom securely exalted, and this goes still farther
in the account.   He was a specimen of the ungodly
characters who hated David for his piety, and his
devotion to the church; brawled, whenever they
dare, in reproach of the king; exulted in his apparent overthrow, and pretended to see the hand
of God in the event, and gloried now that Absalom was to take the kingdom.   How strangely
blended were cursing and blessing in the same
breath!   Cursing the king, and rejoicing that the
Lord had set up Absalom!   It sometimes suits the
basest men to profess an acknowledgment of God's
authority in the government.   This man seems to
have the notion that Absalom would restore the

house of Saul. Very probably the prince had promised that he would grant large favours to all that
fallen party. When the wicked should rule the
vilest men would be exalted.

This sneaking, cowardly hurling of curses and
stones at the king and his servants roused the indignation of Abishai. Like a genuine son of Zeruiah, he felt an impulse to shed blood, and he
begged the privilege of going over and taking off
the venomous scoundrel's head. So dead a dog
should not howl at the king, nor gratify Absalom
with the boast of his valiant insult. But David
took the reproach to his own heart, perhaps with a
painful remembrance that because he was a "man
of blood," the Lord would not permit him to rear
the temple which he had proposed to build. And
he would not allow short vengeance to be taken on
the graceless rebel. Even this reproach was but a
feather added to the burden already imposed upon
him by his own son. Shimei was excited by Absalom's baser treason, and the Lord had permitted
him to curse the king. "Behold my son seeketh
my life, how much more may this Benjaminite do
it ? Let him alone, and let him curse, for the Lord
hath bidden him. It may be that the Lord will
look on mine affliction—" my tearful eye as the
original indicates—" and requite me good for his
cursing this day." Not requite Shimei evil ! This
he does not think of, in his submission to reproach.
And the more heavy the burden the sooner will the

Lord lift it. It was the cursing that cut deepest, and Shimei might follow on, like a cowardly reviler, hurling stones and "dusting him with dust," as long as it would afford him any satisfaction.

This was not probably the first, and certainly not the last man who threw dust into the air as a sign of disrespect, rage, or vindictive malice. The enemies of the Apostle Paul did the same thing when they cried out "Away with such a fellow from the earth: for it is not fit that he should live." (Acts xxii. 22, 23.) Among the Orientals, those, who demand that any one shall be punished threw dust into the air to show that he should be put into his grave. The Turks and Persians utter this curse, "Be covered with earth," or, "Earth be upon thy head." But without the dust, Shimei's crime was great enough. In the law it was written, "Thou shalt not revile the gods (the judges,) nor curse the ruler of thy people."* If he were the last of those who reviled the rulers of a people, humanity would have a better record. There are still those who abuse men in authority,

---

* Exodus xxii. 28, which Fairbairn thus renders: "'Thou shalt not revile God, (not gods, as in our version,) nor curse the ruler of thy people,'—where the visible representative of God is coupled with God himself, and the offence committed against the one is held to be a dishonour to the other. It is precisely in the same way that the honouring of parents is placed among the things due to God himself." Paul speaks of all rulers from the sovereign down to the tax-gatherers as "the ministers of God," who should be obeyed in all their lawful offices. Resistance to them is a form of rebellion against God, who ordained all civil government.

and keep before the public any story that can be
made a scandal or a slander. He however had
this in his favour. He cursed the king to his face.
They speak far out his hearing, or write anony-
mously in a corner. They have not the brazen im-
pudence of the young men who mocked the prophet
Elisha, but they have an equal degree of disrespect
for judges, rulers, and the ministers of truth. Personal abuse has become a considerable part of the
capital in politics. The press is not slow in fur-
nishing the required amount of stock-in-trade for
every party campaign. Every candidate must be
thoroughly abused, and the man who is elected to
an important office is still further abused. The
office itself falls into disrespect. The contagion
spreads, until a people may have little regard for
"the powers that be." From bitter reproaching
there is but a step to clamorous discontent and
turbulent rioting. Those who began with murmur-
ing against Moses, ended their schemes in conspiracy and revolt. Men first declaim against the
ruler, then against the government, then wish for
new laws, and then rebel against the old authority.
One such a man can raise a party of followers, as
Shimei drew to him a thousand Benjaminites, all
eager to help Absalom into power. This abuse of
the tongue and pen has been the curse of all nations. It has not been averted from us. And we
need to know the moral principle of the law—
"Thou shalt not speak evil of the ruler of thy peo-

15

ple." Our Lord boldly declared his mind against great evils, but he never denounced the wicked rulers of the land. The apostles owed few thanks to men in national power, yet, not a disrespectful word fell from their lips or pen. Peter and Jude portray the black character and the heavy doom of those who "despise dominion," and "speak evil of dignities." They were a dangerous class of men, with whom a Christian must not be identified. It is a certain proof that men are far astray from sound morality when they revile their rulers, and make politics consist largely in slandering those whom they cannot defeat by fair arguments. The discussion of measures is the true ground for politics; not the defamation of men. By the first we may have good, honest politicians,—by the second only demagogues. It will be well with us when each can say,

> I am no party man;
> I care for measures more than men, but think
> Some little may depend upon the men;
> Something in fires depend upon the grate.

Notice how the king who had wept in the morning, slept at night, for these late events occurred during the first day's march.

At some point beyond Bahurim—Josephus makes it the banks of the Jordan—there was a halt, "and the king, and all the people that were with him, came weary, and refreshed themselves there."

The soldiers must have carried short rations with them, and the people scarcely enough for their "little ones." Ziba's two hundred loaves of bread, and an hundred bunches of raisins, and an hundred of summer fruits, and a bottle of wine, must have proved a timely present. He was a raven at heart, but even ravens may feed prophets, and he had furnished a table in the wilderness. No doubt David gave thanks for the kind providence. We may well believe that prayer and praise were an important part in the refreshment. It seems that the party rested here until most of the night passed. May we not suppose that here is the place for that "Psalm of David, when he fled from Absalom his son?" If this be so, then what trust in God! No victory yet, no hopeful tidings from Jerusalem; still he has songs in the night, and afterwards can say of those fearful hours, "I cried unto the Lord with my voice, and he heard me out of his holy hill. I laid me down and slept; I awaked, for the Lord sustained me. I will not be afraid of ten thousands of people that have set themselves against me round about."

The faithful can be truly fearless. Piety and courage are as cause and effect. Whom Heaven defends, earth cannot harm. While Absalom was carousing, or sitting proud in his godless council, David was asleep. Peter was in prison bound with two chains, placed between two soldiers, and the object of interest to earth, hell, and heaven;

and while enemies were threatening, friends praying, and an angel coming, Peter was sleeping! And how, between the weeping and the sleeping, he must have cast his burden on the Lord!

> Of all the thoughts of God that are
> Borne upward unto minds afar,
> > Along the Psalmist's music deep—
> Now tell me if that any is
> For gift or grace surpassing this—
> > "He giveth his beloved sleep!"

NOTE.—It has been supposed that the following Psalms were composed by David during the rebellion of Absalom, or shortly after it, and certainly the events of this period and these Psalms throw light upon each other: Ps. iii., iv., v., xl., xlii., xliii., xliv., lv. lxii., lxx., lxxi., cxliii., cxliv.

If this supposition be admitted, (and with great caution too,) we see David a greater literary man in camp than Xenophon or Julius Cæsar, for they penned the mere journal of events; but he drew nobler thoughts from heaven, because he held communion with God.

CHAPTER XIV.

David's Friend, the Orator.

His tongue
Dropped manna, and could make the worse appear
The better reason, to perplex and dash
Maturest counsels.

It is often said that Paris is France. In the same sense Jerusalem was Judea. Thither the tribes went up, and there the power of the government was concentrated. The importance of speedily seizing the capital was manifest to Absalom, especially when the wise Ahithophel was with him to help him appreciate it. If the rebel prince made Hebron his head-quarters, and seat of power, he would appear to be simply at the head of a revolt. But if he established himself at Jerusalem, he would appear to be at the head of the government. The capital being in his hands, he would be recognized by the nation and all its neighbours, as the reigning king. He would have the throne, the tabernacle, the law, and everything belonging to the state and the church in his possession.

Absalom has entered the capital; found it de-

15 *

serted by his father, and is receiving the congratulations and allegiance of his friends. He is surprised that so good a man, and so fast a friend to David as Hushai the Archite should greet him, saying, "God save the king!" Perhaps he means the old king, and he is asked, "Is this thy kindness to thy friend? Why wentest thou not with thy friend?"* At first Hushai seems about to reply with a mental reservation, having on his lips an allegiance to Absalom, but in his mind an allegiance to David. Some readers would like to find it so, but this would not mend the matter. It would be only doubling the deception. Hushai's words grow stronger as he proceeds—perhaps stronger than he first meant to express. Being driven into a corner, he makes an unreserved avowal of subjection to the usurper. Absalom is deceived by what is often called shrewd policy, skilful management of human nature, expediency, and ingenuity. It was making the end justify the means, and doing evil that good might come. Our sympathies go with Hushai, but conscience must not sanction all his conduct. Absalom is more than satisfied, for if so good a man, as

---

* We could hardly expect Absalom to say, "my father." There was a reason for saying "thy friend." It would test Hushai's sincerity by reminding him of his former intimacy with David. There was a time when "Ahithophel was the king's counsellor, and Hushai the Archite was the King's companion." If the one had been nearest David's ear, the other was nearest his heart. The questions asked were pungent and prying.

"David's friend," was joining the infidel standard,
he might hope for all the foes to David's piety,
and all the haters of the Lord.   And now "David's friend" has gained a right to have a voice in
all the deliberations of the burdened hour.

The night is coming.   If the evening sacrifices
are being offered, Absalom does not attend them.
Usurpers have sometimes paid their first devotions
at the altar, thanking God for the success of their
treason, but not so Absalom.   He is, doubtless, in
the "house of cedar," anxious and impatient.   His
father is not his prisoner, nor his victim.   He
must, in some way, make an end of David.   Everything depends on the hour.   He calls a council—
"the first cabinet council to which history admits
us."   We enter it.   It is awfully ungodly, and the
coolness in proposing abominable wickedness, shows
a close familiarity with sin.   Its genius is Ahithophel, and he proposes a course so revolting that we
wonder, more than ever, that he should have been
the counsellor of David.   He is the grandfather of
Bath-sheba, (compare 2 Sam. xi. 3; xxiii. 34,)
and it has been suggested that he intends to be re-
venged on David for the injury once done to her,
by putting Absalom upon a similar course of conduct.   The king's house must be ravaged.   The
deed will enrage the father beyond all prospect of
reconciliation.   It will separate the father and the
son for ever, for Absalom will be held in utter abhorrence.   It will divide the people into two par-

ties, and every man must take a side in the contest. None can remain neutral; none be conservative; very few will dare adhere to David, and the party of Absalom will grow strong. The counsellor hopes much from the ungodliness of the people. The usurper hung not upon the advice, nor had a fear lest all Israel should turn from him in utter disgust and execration. He followed it, and his flatterers approved the abhorrent crime, as a prelude to his kingly administration.

The next piece of Ahithophel's counsel is more worthy of the man who had stood high in David's estimation as a strategist. He advises just what a sagacious warrior, intent upon making a short war, would regard the most prudent. As the one main object is to destroy David's power, Ahithophel sees the surest and shortest way to do it. Out of the multitudes who had flocked to Absalom, let him have twelve thousand of the best, give him the command, and while the prince is rioting, he will this very night make swift pursuit, come upon the king while he is weary and weak-handed; and in his fright he cannot resist; the people will flee, and only David will be smitten. Then the people can be persuaded to submit to the new king in peace.

This counsel pleased Absalom well, and all the elders of Israel. We do not wonder. From their point of view the advantages of the plan were many and striking. It was prompt, brought the war into a small compass, seemed certain of success, and would avoid a general and unpopular slaughter. It would not put Absalom's precious life in peril, and would force decision upon all who were yet inclined to loyalty. Our only wonder is that the council were willing to listen to any other proposal, or reject this plan after hearing it. But God was overruling and restraining the wrath of man. "He taketh the wise in their own craftiness." The scale is to be turned by the power of words.

It seems that Hushai had not heard the brief speech of Ahithophel. Perhaps he was so shocked by the first advice of this renegade statesman, that he shrank back from the council. Absalom had him called, told him the plan, and probably expecting nothing but a strong second to it, asked his advice. It was a moment of intense anxiety to "David's friend." Never, perhaps, in the history of eloquence, was an orator so beset with difficulties and dangers. Violent and reckless men are all around him. The chief counsellor can easily suspect and ferret out a spy. A word, a syllable, a breath, a gesture, a glance, may betray him. To oppose one who has been in Israel as "the oracle of God," is almost folly. To speak a word for David is perilous; he may bring ruin upon his master's cause, and forfeit his own life.

But something must be done. Now or never must he be of service to his king. David can be captured without a doubt. He saw him "weary and weak-handed," in tears and alarm, only a few hours ago, with a weeping train of followers who would be helpless in a night-attack. Before the morrow's sun the king and the kingdom may perish together. He however is blessed with penetration and wit equally with the old counsellor. His object is to gain time enough for David to cross the Jordan. And now he sets earnestly, yet deliberately about it. He must not sharply oppose Ahithophel, must not excite a discussion, must not allow the plan to be brought up again, but must drive it out of the minds of his hearers by impressive words. He must excite the imagination of his hearers. He must take Ahithophel by a sort of mental generalship, equal to the oracle's military skill. And he does it. He rouses memories of David's courage, guardedness, and victory. He reminds them that David is not the man to be caught asleep, nor to be negligent of strategy. He will be hidden just where nobody expects him, and of all times to be on his track, the night is the worst. The flight may be on the wrong side for Absalom, if his men venture to the door of the lion's den. And then, appealing to Absalom's excessive vanity, he paints the glory of his going forth himself as the commanding general, with all Israel in battle array. Delay will make the prince glorious, and his grandeur will carry the whole nation with him by enthusiasm.

"And Hushai said, The counsel that Ahithophel has given is not good at this time (however good in

general.) For thou knowest thy father and his men,
that they be, said Hushai, mighty men, and they be
(even now) chafed in their minds as a bear robbed
of her whelps in the field : and thy father is a man
of war, and will not lodge with the people (exposed
and unguarded).   Behold, he is hid now in some
pit, or in some other place (well defended) ; and it
will come to pass, when some of them (who are
proposed to be sent after him this night) be over-
thrown at the first, that (a panic will ensue, and)
whosoever heareth it will say, There is a slaughter
among the people that follow Absalom.   And (then)
he also that is valiant, whose heart is as the heart
of a lion, shall utterly melt : for all Israel knoweth
that thy father is a mighty man, and they which be
with him are valiant men.   (They are not the men
to flee and let David be captured.)   Therefore I
counsel, that all Israel be generally gathered unto
thee, from Dan even to Beer-sheba, as the sand that
is by the sea for multitude ; and that thou go to
battle in thine own person, (getting to thyself all
the glory of a great campaign and victory.)   So
shall we come upon him in some place where he
shall be found, and we will light upon him as the
dew falleth on the ground : and of him and of all
the men that are with him there shall not be left
so much as one.   Moreover if he be gotten into a
city, then shall all Israel bring ropes to that city,
and we will draw it into the river, until there be
not one small stone found there."

The effect of this short speech was overpowering; the triumph complete. Hushai's counsel was at once declared the wiser, because it seemed that the carrying out of his proposed plan would thoroughly exterminate David and his party, and increase the royal dignity of Absalom by the splendours of a military achievement. One secret of the orator's success was, that Satan had outwitted himself in preparing Absalom for the work of rebellion, and in instilling into him an unbounded self-importance. His overweening vanity had led him astray, and now, in a twinkling, he is so flattered with the hope of glory that he gives up the very policy which appeared most sure of success. But the great reason was, that God was calmly swaying the movements of men and devils, and defeating the schemes of His enemies. While he could not approve the deception of Hushai, he made use of it for good. Hence the great secret of the orator's success was that "the Lord had appointed to defeat the good (or wise) counsel of Ahithophel, to the intent that the Lord might bring evil upon Absalom." He made this eloquent speech the pivot on which turned the destiny of the usurper, and the restoration of the Lord's anointed. He that sat in the heavens laughed, and held the rebels in derision, for he would again set his king upon the holy hill of Zion.

Ahithophel is dumb with astonishment at the blindness of the prince and the cabinet. They act like fools, in rejecting his proposals. Their cause is lost, by giving David one night more time, and he will have nothing to do with such a dallying council. They are not worthy of such an oracle as he is, and he will make them know the want of him. Failure must come, and he will not remain to bear the disgrace of defeat, nor endure death for treason. Mortally offended, he rides home, instead of riding forth to capture David. One would think that he would wait to see the result, and at least have the satisfaction of saying, "I knew it—I told you so! If I could have had my way, all this would never have occurred!" But he cannot endure the slur cast upon his wisdom and his generalship. Not the approaching ruin of the cause, so much as the personal affront to himself, preys upon his mind. He resolves to take his own life. Mad enough to hang himself, he is yet wise enough to set his house in order before he does it. He may not be the first man who hanged himself, but "he bears the unenviable distinction of being the first whose hanging himself is recorded." Like Judas, he went to "his own place."

"What a contrast to David in his power of bearing disgrace! Men of the richest natural gifts have often proved wofully deficient in self-control: the list of suicides contains the names of some of the most gifted of men. Only special grace can impart the power to stand erect under

16

the bewildering humiliations and reverses of the
world.   How vain is it for a man to be wise, if he
be not wise in God !''   The voice of the gospel to
every one in troubles which tempt to desperation,
is, "Do thyself no harm.   Believe on the Lord
Jesus Christ, and thou shalt be saved.''

For some reason Hushai does not feel perfectly
sure that his counsel will be followed.   How trust
the traitors ?   When their imaginations cool they
may revert to the measure first proposed, and dash
forth to waylay the king.   At best only a breath-
ing-time is secured to David.   The danger is not
removed ; the crisis is simply delayed.   He therefore prudently informs the priests, Zadok and
Abiathar, of the advice given on both sides.   They
are prepared for the emergency.   Each has a son
hiding outside of the city, at En-rogel, (supposed
by some to be the later "Fountain of Siloam.")   A
maid-servant bears to them the message, and they
convey it to David, saying, "Lodge not this night
in the plains of the wilderness, but speedily pass
over (the Jordan ;) lest the king be swallowed up,
and all the people that are with him.''

Even the lads of the neighbourhood were affected
with a mania for Absalom, the prince with the
long hair, the gay horses, and the gilded chariots.
One of them saw the sons of the priests, suspected
their mission to the king, and with boyish officious-
ness hasted to Absalom, as glad to have something
to tell, as he was to hear it.   He ordered his ser-

vants to intercept the despatches. The wonder is
that he did not fall upon the priests, but God protected them. Bahurim had some good people in
it, who were not drawn away into the errors of
Shimei, and an excellent well for a hiding-place.
The young messengers went down into the well,
and the good woman, more loyal than candid,
cunningly spread a covering over the well, and put
ground corn upon it, as if she had been airing it,
and was carelessly leaving it out rather late in the
evening. The pursuers came, inquired for Ahimaaz
and Jonathan, and thinking the woman to be an
artless creature, believed her when she said "they
be gone over the brook of water." They searched
the premises, and, supposing that if she had not
sense enough to take care of her corn, she had not
wit enough to hide the messengers, they perhaps
jestingly told her that the dew would not help it
any, and returned to the city. The woman, in the
spirit of the honoured Rahab, watched her time, un-
sealed the well, and bade the trusty messengers
good-speed. Her false statement cannot be justified, but we must acknowledge the important part
she performed in securing the safety of David.
She was one of the nameless ones, still loyal to her
rightful king.

Who knows but that the king was sleeping when
the message was brought into his camp? He understood it, arose, roused the people, and they
passed over the river. "By the morning light

there lacked not one of them that was not gone over Jordan." The "little ones" whom the noble captain, Ittai, had been so careful of at the Kedron, were doubtless carried over in the same kind way. None were lost in crossing or fording the river. Here some draw a parallel between David and Christ who said in a difficult day, "Of all that thou hast given me, have I lost none." We have often reason to notice David's tender care for all who trusted him for safety in their distresses.

CHAPTER XV.

The King's Head-Quarters.

That man
May safely venture to go on his way
That is so guided that he cannot stray.

THE Lord had stirred up the eagle's nest, but was bearing David on eagles' wings to himself and to a place which he had made sacred by his presence. While every movement of the rebel prince is a blunder, every step that the king takes is one of wisdom. He is guided by. an unseen hand to Mahanaim. Near it Jacob had wrestled with the angel, and called the place Peniel, because he had there seen God face to face, and his life had been preserved. We may believe that David's prayers are worthy of the place, and when needing wisdom, it is liberally given him of God. It is wise for him to make Mahanaim his head-quarters. As a "base of military operations," none could be better. The forty miles between it and Jerusalem could not be made in a night's march by the rebel army. Its defences and its nearness to supplies had commended it to Ishbosheth and Abner, when

16 *

they attempted to maintain the crown in the house
of Saul. It is wise to tempt Absalom across the
Jordan, and draw the battle toward a wood where
the arms of giant oaks are reaching forth to seize
the chief conspirator. Long ago God placed the
oak there to fulfil his purposes of justice. It is
wise to be in a pastoral region, where the prime ·
articles of food are abundant, and where brave and
hardy men, attached to their family-chiefs, and
loyal to their king, will be ready to come at the
call of their leaders, and add their strength to the
royal army. We know not the men thus furnished, but the generosity of three of these chieftains is touchingly recorded.

We have all heard of the men who were ordered
to remain at Jericho, until their beards were grown.
They were not striplings, whose pretensions to man-
liness were in advance of their years, but dignified
ambassadors, men of rank and station, who had
been grossly insulted by Hanun the son of Nahash.
This Nahash, cruel enough usually, had been kind
to David, who was the last man to forget a favour.
Hanun lost his father some years after, and became a pompous king in a petty kingdom. David,
remembering the old kindness, sent certain noble-
men to express his sympathies to the new king.
But Hanun treated them as spies, cut off the skirts
of their robes, and shaved off half their beards—a
thing regarded as worse than a complete shaving.
King David knew how ridiculous they would ap-

pear in this wretched plight, and in tender regard for their feelings, sent them word to tarry at Jericho until their beards should grow respectably long for a public appearance. War followed, and Hanun had reason to come to that sort of repentance which men feel when they are forced to recall their sins because they must reap the consequences. It could hardly be expected that any relative of Hanun would be kind to David. Yet his own brother Shobi comes to the head-quarters, loaded with supplies for the army.

One would scarcely suppose that the lame boy, Mephibosheth, had anything good to say of David when he was growing up in the house of Machir of Lo-debar. The guardian, in pitying the lame child, might have hated him whom Saul held as an enemy. Yet Machir comes of his own accord, with gifts prompted by the noblest patriotism. And good old Barzillai—we expect him to come, for he is rich in loyalty, and loyal with his wealth. Sanitary and Christian commissions are of no modern date, for these leading men of Gilead "brought beds, and basins, and earthen vessels, and wheat, and barley, and flour, and parched corn, and beans, and lentiles, and parched pulse, and honey—" one almost wishes he had been there as the list lengthens—" and butter, and sheep, and cheese of kine, for David and for the people that were with him, to eat; for they said, The people is hungry, and weary, and thirsty in the wilderness." The burden of supplying an army with rations is a very serious one, and David not only finds it lifted, but his heart is lightened, for "A generous soul is sunshine to the mind." He has been guided into this region of rich farms and loyal hearts by the good hand of God.

It is also wise in David, while hoping for the best to prepare for the worst. War must come; terrible war of the son against the father, and brother against brother. It is a tremendous necessity. The rebellion is not a thing of words, and he cannot by mere words allay it. It is an armed rebellion, and the only possible resort for him is to set an armed force against it. The only way to a good peace is through a good war. And he has wisdom for the emergency. According to the rather doubtful testimony of Josephus, the entire number does not, however, exceed four thousand men. The crafty general Joab, has come, and in a trying time he is an host in himself. Abishai, did not turn back offended, when David said to him, at his proposal to take the head off Shimei, "What have I to do with you, ye sons of Zeruiah!" He is present, cool enough to command.

With his remarkable talent for military arrangement, David puts his forces into three brigades, with an eminent general over each. He proposes to head the entire force, and share in the perils of the fight. "I will surely go forth with you myself also." The smaller his army, the more need of him whose aged hand can still hold firm the sword. "But the people answered, Thou shalt not go forth; for if we flee away they will not care for us; neither if half of us die, will they care for us; but now thou art worth ten thousand of us; therefore, now it is better that thou succour us out of (or from) the city." The voice of the people was, in this instance, the voice of God, and he said, "What seemeth you best, I will do."

David had all this wisdom, no doubt, in answer to prayer. We should notice it, because there lurks in the minds of some persons, an idea that if good sense be not naturally possessed, it is useless to pray for it. Very certain is it that sound discretion is one of the blessings which we are invited to ask. "If any man lack wisdom let him ask of God."

When the hour came for the battle, "the king stood by the gate-side (of Mahanaim) and all the people came out by hundreds and by thousands." Every company, regiment, and brigade, was marshalled in order, and we leave the king reviewing his army, to trace the march of the young man Absalom.

CHAPTER XVI.

The Rebels Marching.

A sceptre snatched with an unruly hand,
Must be as boist'rously maintained as gained.

THE wisest thing for Absalom would have been
to remain in Jerusalem, fortify it, raise an army,
and put himself on the defensive; then declare
that he was not seeking war, but only asking to be
let alone. If the king attacked him he could
charge on him the blame of the first blow, and with
pretended horror cry out against the inhumanity
of a father in making war upon a son. How plausible the assertion that his father was "A man of
blood," and he a man of peace!

The character, the designs and the conduct of
Absalom are by no means worthy of being brought
beside those of William III. when he assumed the
right to take the throne of England, peaceably if
he could, by war if he must. But Absalom's folly
may be illustrated by William's policy. James
had fled from the throne in cowardice. William
did not make war against him, pursuing him to the

death. He let him wander where he chose in
peace. The people began to appreciate the leniency, and acknowledge the rights of the new king.
James had no other way but to begin the war, attack the coasts, and invade the kingdom. When
he made the attempt, the people generally regarded
him as the aggressor, and resisted, or drove him
from the soil. They repelled his son Prince Charles,
in the same spirit. The crown was settled upon
the house of Orange, and the Stuarts were forever
excluded from the throne. A similar policy with
Absalom, might have produced similar results. But
God had not left his theocracy thus to be over-
turned. The usurper was allowed to act unwisely,
and indulge the pretensions of a rebel and the cruelties of a son, for thus he would work his own defeat and ruin.

In his impatience to make the throne secure, he
was not content to drive the king into the remotest
corner of the realm, but he must chase him out of
the world. There might still be magic in the name
of David, and hearts longing for his restoration.
A rebel cannot have strong faith in other rebels,
nor even in himself. Those to-day most enthu-
siastic for the prince, may wish to-morrow to return
to their former allegiance. Blindness, in part,
hath happened to Israel, because he has hood-
winked and befooled the people. Their eyes may
soon be opened, and then he must become their detestation. They will see his intrigues, read his

black heart through and through, despise the traitor, shake off his yoke of tyranny and call back
the rightful king to the throne.   There must be no
king to call back, and therefore he makes ready for
the war against the father.

How nearly his army came to the vast one "as
the sand that is by the sea for multitude," pre-
sented to his imagination by "David's friend," we
cannot tell.   There must have been . over twenty
thousand; Josephus says, "many ten thousands."
If on the first evening the rebels entered the capital, the numbers were so great that Ahithophel could
"choose out twelve thousand men," the rapid gathering of forces for three or four days would swell
them to a vast array.   The difficulty of raising a
large army in a short time may not have been so
great as we imagine.   Saul, at a time when he was
unpopular, summoned an army for the relief of Ja-
besh-Gilead, and in four or five days had three
hundred and thirty thousand men of war.   It was
at a period when there were no professional soldiers, no organized troops of militia.   Every man
was, however, familiar with the use of weapons,
from his youth, and ready at a moment's call to
leave the flock or field, and march against the
enemy.   Every man took his "rations" with him
from home, and lessened the public burden of fur-
nishing supplies.   If his knapsack was exhausted,
he lived on love for his country until something
could be provided.   The call for troops was con-

veyed by swift runners, or telegraphed by signal-fires kindled one after another on the mountains. Such a call may have gone forth from Hebron when Absalom took possession of it, and if so, the men of the stolen hearts needed but a short time to report themselves in Jerusalem. It was like the old Scottish chiefs summoning their clans when war was suddenly opening to them an inviting field.

So extended was the rebellion, that it is not represented as a local or party uprising, but as a great national revolt. Engaged in it were "all the people, the men of Israel," "all the elders of Israel." And the term *Israel* did not yet mean only the ten tribes, but the whole nation. The small numbers with David, or secretly loyal at their homes, formed but an exception to the general revolt. Inflated now with vanity, proud of his success, and drunk with ambition for the glory of leading such an army to victory, Absalom assumed the chief command, forgetting that he who has never served knows not how to govern. He led his forces out of the city, and very likely the cowardly Shimei hailed him with a blessing as he passed. Crossing the Jordan, he pitched in the land of Gilead.

"And Absalom made Amasa captain of the host instead of Joab." He had, perhaps, expected Joab to join in the rebellion, and held for him this appointment. We may find something to account, in part, for the presence of Amasa among the rebels,

17

although he was a nephew of king David, and
Joab's cousin. David had a sister Abigail, who
married Jether an Ishmaelite (1 Chron. ii. 17), or
after changing his nationality and, perhaps, his religion, he was called Ithra an Israelite (2 Sam.
xvii. 25.) This man seems not to have stood very
high in the king's estimation. Amasa, the son,
was therefore neglected, while his cousins, the sons
of Zeruiah, were promoted to great honour and influence. No doubt he thought himself as good as
any nephew of the king, and the slight was hard to
bear. . If, therefore, David's hand had been against
him, barring the way to preferment, his own Ishmaelite hand should now be against David. An
office-seeker has not much conscience to feel the
sin of rebellion.

Ambition's eyes
Look often higher than their merits rise.

While the battle is drawing nigh, and the scouts
are exploring the country, we may notice some of
its features. In the tribe of Gad is a large forest
called the "wood of Ephraim." How it came to
bear the name of a tribe on the other side of the
river is not known. Some think, because of the
slaughter of the Ephraimites on this spot, in the
time of Jephthah, (Judges xii. 4–6,) when blood
enough was shed to make it worthy of the title.
May it not have been so called because certain
"fugitives from Ephraim" had settled there, and
fixed their name upon it, to remain long after they

suffered for the slight difference between "Shibbo-
leth" and "Sibboleth"? It had been a battle-
ground, where armies fought, not about words, but
for great principles, and was to be again, when the
test-words should be loyalty and rebellion. Not
far distant, Og the giant once flourished, and may
have bowed to save his towering head from the
hanging boughs of the oaks of Bashan. As an oak
is to perform a conspicuous part in bringing about
the end of Absalom and his rebellion, we may notice it here. Tradition does not assume to point
out the exact tree, but modern critics, who have a
fondness for making changes in our English Bible,
make war upon the word *oak*, and insist that it
should be *terebinth*. It matters little to us which
it was, except for the sake of keeping people from
going so far in their uncertainties, that they will
think it no matter whether Absalom was caught at
all by the boughs of a tree. In the "Land and
the Book," the traveller and author is very zealous
for the *oak*, although it is *alah* instead of *allon* in
the original. He says, "that battle-field was on
the mountains east of the Jordan, always celebrated
for great oaks—not for terebinths. The name
'wood of Ephraim' signifies a wild, rocky region,
overgrown with trees, mostly oak, *never* the terebinth. There is no such thing in this country as a
terebinth-wood. Yet this *alah*, which caught Absalom, formed part of the wood of Ephraim. It
was an oak, I firmly believe. There are thousands

of such trees still in the same country, admirably
suited to catch long-haired rebels, but no terebinths.
Indeed this latter does not meet the requirements
of the catastrophe at all.   I see it asserted by the
advocates of this translation that the oak is not a
common nor a very striking tree in this country, implying that the terebinth is.   A greater
mistake could scarcely be made.   As to strength,
it is simply ridiculous to compare the terebinth
with the oak, and the same in regard to size.   Still
more surprising are the statements about the extent of oak forests in this land.   Why there are more
mighty oaks here in this immediate vicinity than
there are terebinths in all Syria and Palestine together." In this skirmish of words the oak is defended with no little of the same loyalty to the
good old English version, that we feel in establish-
ing the firm allegiance of Joab to his king.   And
this brave old general is now about to take his position in or near the "wood of Ephraim," to wait
for the rebel army to advance and open the battle.
A good position is half the victory.

CHAPTER XVII.

Deal Gently.

Dost thou deem
It such an easy task from the fond heart
To root affection out?

THE dreaded day has come at last. And the battle must be fought. The hour for the march to the forest can no longer be delayed, lest the rebel forces bring their engines and their ropes, and attempt such a siege as "David's friend" had persuaded Absalom would be glorious, and all the horrors of carnage be carried into the streets and homes of the city. Well may the excited inhabitants of Mahanaim thank David that he does not defend himself behind its walls. The moment has come when the captains wait for their orders, and the father must give them, though every word be aimed at his son. Agitated he stands by the gate side, and as the troops file by almost in silence, they hear him say to each of his three generals, "Deal gently, for my sake, with the young man, even with Absalom."

No fears for the result, no hopelessness of vic-

17 *

tory, no thought of how the young man would deal with him should he get him in his power, not a doubt but the prince will be overcome, and probably captured, no trembling for the ark of God sent back to risk the desecration of the ungodly; but only the thought of his son's exposure to injury and death, and his own pangs of heart should he be slain. And as the thirsty soldiers in a dreary wilderness are permitted to linger a moment and drink of the brook by the way, so let us again be refreshed by the stream of paternal love so often met with in our progress through David's history.

We are altogether wrong in our theology, our faith, and our practical life, if we suppose that justice and mercy are opposing attributes. One does not exclude the other. One takes the form of law, the other clothes itself in love. One gives us a hatred of sin, the other imparts a love for the sinner. One shows us that punishment is right, the other prompts us to redeem the guilty from punishment. Justice forbids that revenge which " looks from the fault to the individual," and says " torture and kill him." It is in perfect unity with that love which " looks from the fault to the individual, and says, pity and save him." Sin is God's abhorrence, and whenever it comes within the reach of human law, it should be punished with just severity. And when it grows into crimes of murder and treason, like those of Absalom, it deserves death. It must be put away from society.

and "to put it away from us, we must slay him who. is fatally infected, and whose infection will spread; but not towards him are we necessitated to entertain any feeling but love; the whole fervour of our hate is against that snake whose deadly venom has utterly tainted his blood."

"And have not men in all ages borne witness to an instinctive feeling of this distinction? Bad as the world is, there perhaps was never a scaffold erected, and a man put to death upon it, for whom, whatever his crime, certain eyes in the crowd were not filled with the dew of pity. * * * * They witnessed to the fact that it is a stern work for man to be the executioner of man. It is the mark of the evil one perceived on a fellow-creature that is hated, not that creature himself. Would to God! men say from their inmost hearts, we could part this evil from you; but we cannot, and we must expel it from the midst of us; you must go with it. The tainted spot must be cut out; but while the knife is being whetted, the tear is being shed." (*Bayne's Christian Life.*)

King David now stands before us in this very attitude. We approve, with all justice, his taking up arms against Absalom. It may be death to his son, but the son deserves it. Should the king go forth against him, and slay him, we could not refuse to call it just. David loves law, order, government, and the nation's peaceful security, and he therefore must punish rebellion. He must wipe out this enormous wickedness, and he knows that Joab will make clear work of it, if it be possible. He does not restrain him from going to the battle. But lest the cold-browed general should temper justice with revenge rather than mercy, he attempts to check his strong passion by saying, " Deal gently." It is the rebellion that he hates, and not the rebel. Pity for Absalom is consistent with an intense hatred of Absalom's crime, and a strong determination to crush it in its rising and threatening power. The sturdiest warrior may weep for his foes, and yet fight them to the death. A tear in Joab's eye would commend him to us as all the nobler in his vigorous justice.

Nor is king David in any new position. Often has he stood with justice and mercy united in his soul. We may see how he looked—and how the God of David looked—upon a righteous government, upon its enemies, and upon war as a necessary means of promoting a government in love, and punishing its foes in severe justice. Christian men of all times have had the serious questions pertaining to war coming up often before them. They have been forced to examine them in the light of the Bible. It may be thus until the millennial day shall dawn. We can never be wiser than the word of God.

Several of the next paragraphs are taken from the author's sermon entitled, "Thanksgiving for victory," published in 1863.

The Bible does not glory in war. The most splendid campaigns of Joshua and David are sketched in the fewest words—often a single verse is crowded with facts that would have made long chapters in Spartan or in Latin history. The very silence about these daring expeditions and dazzling victories is a small proof of the inspiration of the Bible. Human nature could not have resisted the temptation to describe great battles, and illustrate the glory of the nation's patriots and the valour of her defenders.

But the Bible is not so silent concerning the feelings of godly and patriotic men toward the enemies who attempted the nation's overthrow. It is not silent concerning the justice that moved them to enter the conflict, nor the thanksgiving to the " God of battles " after their triumph had been won. We could not understand these feelings, nor these thanksgivings, if we had no experience of war, nor of victory.

There are, in the Bible, things which we are now prepared to understand more fully than in the days of peace. If certain feelings of men were wrong, we need to know their error and avoid it, and hush our thanksgivings for victory. If they were right —if in their severity they were just, we need to appreciate the reason.

You have found in David's Psalms "some things hard to be understood." David was a man of mercy. He was no cruel, revengeful, and unrelenting despot. But as a king he was a man of justice. There was a righteousness that filled his soul with judgment upon the enemies of the government of which he was the administrator. He did not stand forth, and with boasting declare his vengeance against them. He submitted his case to God. He breathed his severest thoughts through prayer, and implored Jehovah to execute justice.

"Arise, O Lord, in thine anger, lift up thyself because of the rage of mine enemies: and awake for me to the judgment that thou hast commanded. —Give them according to their deeds, and according to the wickedness of their endeavours: give them after the work of their own hands; render to them their desert.—Destroy thou them, O God; let them fall by their own counsels; cast thou them out in the multitude of their transgressions; for they have rebelled against thee."

Dr. Duff, the celebrated Scottish Missionary in Calcutta, said that he could not understand how these deprecatory prayers were consistent with the teachings of the New Testament, until the Sepoy rebellion broke out with such terrific fury, and foes rose up filling the land with violence, shaking the foundations of government, threatening towns and cities with fire and sword, murdering the innocent, persecuting Christians with especial cruelty, making resistless missionaries a sacrifice to brutal lust and deathly torture, and rolling back the tide of Christian civilization, that iniquity might come in again like a flood, and heathenism be re-established with all the horrors of barbarism and idolatry. Only then could it be known that there are times in the outbreaking of human enmity when the pleadings of mercy are in vain, and Justice must draw the sword for a vigorous war of self-defence.

These expressions of David, when rightly understood, have never excited or encouraged the spirit of revenge.—They are no more fitted to have such an effect than the severe sentence of justice pronounced by a judge, or the act of an officer who executes the penalties of death.—Even these denunciations are not absolute. They are submitted to a righteous God, and are suspended on the enemy's persistence in opposition, or his repentance and his cessation from deeds of injustice.

Yet why these feelings toward enemies? The fact of their being natural to human nature might condemn them. The reason is plain. They were not simply David's enemies, nor were their opposition and injustice merely a personal matter with him. If so, he was the very man to have prayed for their pardon and to have forgiven them. For mercy and forgiveness towards his personal foes, were distinguishing traits of his character. But these foes were the enemies of God. They were the haters of the Lord. They had risen up against the government which Jehovah had established. They sought to break the union of the tribes and states of Israel. To war against the Theocracy was to fight against God. And hence he could consistently say in his appeal to Jehovah—

"Thine hand shall find out all thine enemies; thy right hand shall find out those that hate thee. Thou shalt make them as a fiery oven in the time of thine anger: the Lord shall swallow them up in his wrath, and the fire shall devour them.—For they intended mischief against thee: they imagined a mischievous device, which they are not able to perform. Therefore thou shalt make them turn their back, when thou shalt make ready thine arrows upon thy strings against the face of them."

And why could David render thanksgiving to God for the defeat or death of his enemies? On what principle could he exult in a tone of solemn triumph, saying, "Thou hast smitten all mine enemies; thou hast broken the teeth of the ungodly. —I have pursued mine enemies, and have overtaken them; neither did I turn again until they were consumed. I beat them small as the dust before the wind?"

No doubt the language has often startled us. It does not seem, at first, quite like the gospel spirit of "peace on earth, and good will to men." But remember, David was seeking peace and righteousness. Only by war could they be gained. They who had taken the sword must perish by the sword. They who would acknowledge no principle but justice upon themselves, must be subdued by judgments. And remember that God had anticipated the fact that these enemies would be submissive to nothing but the power of military justice. On account of their sins, he had declared against them a war of subjugation, and if that were not enough, a war of extermination. David, therefore, thought it his duty to sweep them away as unsparingly and as thoroughly as a benevolent man would clear away the elements of a pestilence.

This justice is a principle about which there is sometimes a feeble sentimentalism that makes even mercy unmeaning, and deprives law of its penalties, and dares to go so far as to deny its power in God's government, and its place among his attributes. Without its proper exercise in our families, our schools, our courts, our government, we shall inevitably come to wreck. It is but another name for an exalted and all-comprehending Love. It is love for all holy truth, for righteousness, for liberty, for just government, and for God who has ordained the powers that exist for the highest national welfare of men. It is a love for order, for peace—a peace that must sometimes be purchased with the sword—a love for union and for brotherhood.

But this is not a love that repeals law, cancels the rights of a government and obliterates justice. God loves all men with an infinite benevolence and compassion, but this does not prevent the infliction of all the severities of just punishment.

18

He loves all holy principles more than he loves those who violate them. When you read his utterances against his enemies, " let it not be imagined that the Being from whom they come is without pity and without love; never would he utter them if a milder course could serve the ends of true benevolence and comprehensive compassion. It is because he sees them to be truly indispensable that he resolves on such dismal severities; but once resolved on, he executes them without shrinking or sign of fear."

We may imitate the Divine love, and still imitate also the Divine justice. We may love the guiltiest criminals according to law, still inflicting upon them, only in a legal manner, the severe penalties they have incurred.

"Christian love is of two kinds—the love of approving complacency, and the love of benevolence. Every human being is entitled to our love of benevolence, or wishing him well, whatever be his character; but it is only those whose character is amiable, who are entitled to our love of approbation and complacency. Applying this distinction to our enemies, we ought to love them with benevolence, or wish them well, though their general character be bad." (*Foote on Luke.*)

" We may love our enemy, and yet have resentment against him for his injurious behaviour toward us. But when this resentment entirely destroys our natural benevolence towards him, it is excessive, and becomes malice or revenge." (*Bp. Butler.*)

With such feelings of justice towards the nation's enemies had King David come to meet the rebellion of Absalom. But never before had there been so great and so aggravated a national crime with which he was compelled to deal. All Israel in revolt at the instigation of one man, and that man his most beloved son! Never before had his merciful heart found it so hard to throw its iron blood into the arm that must be raised to inflict a righteous punishment. Never before was his justice so tempered with mercy. Never before had he been constrained by affection for the guilty to say "deal gently." In loyalty and with respect for the "Lord's anointed" he had spared Saul when he had him in his power. But now in the same loyalty and with the same respect for the anointing of the Lord, he must send forth his army to conquer the rebellious Absalom. How his heart passes over the hateful sin, and fixes in compassion on the son!

Many have thought that King David was carried away too far by the impulses of paternal affection. They do not sympathize with his "deal gently." They regard it as arising from a misdirected love, and a compromising pity. They think that his gentle dealing would have been unjust to the government and to the few loyal men who had not yet bowed to Absalom. They are surprised to hear the righteous David, heretofore so rigid in his justice, saying, "deal gently." And Bishop Hall in astonishment exclaims, "O holy David, what means this ill-placed love, this unjust mercy? Deal gently with a traitor! that traitor a son! that son an Absalom! the graceless darling of so good a father! and this for *thy* sake, whose crown he has usurped, whose blood he is thirsting after! For whose sake should Absalom be *pursued*, if he is spared for thine? He was courteous to thy followers—affable and plausible to all Israel,—cruel and implacable only to thee! And yet thou sayest, 'Deal gently with the young man Absalom, for my sake.'"

But remember, David has provided for the satisfaction which the government requires. He has sent his army to conquer and blot out rebellion. He has commissioned the sword to secure an atonement by blood, and hoping that the great crime of the nation will meet with the justice which the laws demand, he would at least save one rebel from the wreck. The one most loved, though guiltiest of all, has the first place in his heart. Let justice be done on a general scale, so that the government shall be satisfied, but spare Absalom "for my sake."

Not for justice's sake—that demands a life twice forfeited, by murder and by treason. Not for the kingdom's sake—that requires an example to be made of the excuseless rebel; not for the law's sake, that can be made honourable only by the satisfaction of death—not for Jehovah's sake, for his decree hangs heavy over the criminal, and cannot be uplifted; not even for mercy's sake, for the extension of mercy is not rightly in the king's power, but *"for my sake."* My life is so much bound up in his, that the blow will fall on me. It will be like death to me. I cannot bear to see him slain. He is too guilty to die, and fall into the hands of the living God. "Deal gently." Beware that none touch the young man Absalom."

Here was a God-like compassion, a Christ-like love. If God pitied us only as justice would measure out compassion toward us, not one of us could be spared. If he dealt with us only for his kingdom's sake, there could be no gentleness. But for his own sake he loves the sinner, even while the sin is his abhorrence. He is greater than his government, for he established it; greater than his laws, for he made them. They exist for his sake, for his glory. He does not overlook them in his love for sinners. He does not cancel them in sparing the guilty. But he, in his unspeakable love, provides for the satisfaction of their demands. An atonement for our sin, our revolt from God, our rebellion against his government, is made by his only-begotten Son whom he sent into the world, and freely offered to us. He invites us to accept it. He deals gently with us to persuade us to re-

18 *

ceive the atonement, and the pardon of all our sins. And what may we plead ? "For thy name's sake"—for the glory of all the attributes which compose thy name—"pardon mine iniquity." "Save me for thy mercies' sake."

It is for his own sake that he deals now with us in gentleness. If his government were all that he regarded, he might make a short work of sin upon earth. To crush this great rebellion against Jehovah, would be less than the work of a day. But to all ministering spirits who have power over sinners, he says "deal gently" with them, though their sins be great. To the sun, bearing his arrows by day and the storms with their arrows by night, he says "deal gently." To the plague, the pestilence, and whole troop of diseases, sent forth to smite sinners, he says "deal gently." To all the powers that be; to all who execute laws; to all who are sent to warn sinners of the wrath to come, he declares in giving them their commissions, "deal gently" with the sons of men. And it may come to pass that by the mercies of God, by the love of Christ, by the tenderness of the Holy Ghost, and by the undeserved favours of a kind Providence, one here, and another there, may be led to turn an eye heavenward, and say with thankful heart, "thy gentleness hath made me great." And multitudes may say, of the Lord, "He hath not dealt with us after our sins, nor rewarded us according to our iniquities. For as the heaven is high above the earth, so great is his mercy toward them that fear him. As far as the east is from the west, so far hath he removed our transgressions from us. Like as a father pitieth his children, so the Lord pitieth them that fear him. For he knoweth our frame, he remembereth that we are dust."

What King David thought of doing with Absalom we know not. But we know that he could have pointed out to his guilty son, the way of atonement, pardon, and peace with God. And this we may all do, when dealing with those whose sins we hate, and may perhaps be called to treat with human punishment. The greater their transgressions, the more pity should we feel for the transgressors, and the more earnestly seek to reclaim them. We should "gaze upon the wandering mortal, however black his iniquity, with eyes wherein every glance of indignation, every dark speck of hatred, every scowl of revenge, is drowned in the softest dew." "Let who will deny the compatibility of a Christian hatred of sin, with a Christian love for the sinner; let it appear to philosophers and natural religionists chimerical or weak as it may; the Christian can always respond by merely pointing to him, (Christ Jesus,) as he appeared on that day when he looked over Jerusalem. Was there infinite hatred of sin in those words of doom? Was there infinite love in those tears? (*Bayne.*)

Or if this be too high an example for us, look to King David, standing by the gate of Mahanaim, and with all the tender feelings of a father, and the pity of a godly man for the guilty, just on the verge of irrecoverable woe, pleading with the flint-faced messengers of justice, "Deal gently, for my sake, with the young man, even with Absalom."

The young man! If any need such pity; if for any there be a plea that God and men would spare; if toward any there should be tenderness, persuasion and a winning loving-kindness, and if on any these may have an influence for everlasting good, he is the young man; any, every young man. Even though he be an Absalom, for whom justice waits, "go speak to that young man." Thy words may be as arrows piercing his sins, and he may go to the Saviour for the healing of his wound.

Think gently of the erring, O, do not thou forget,
However darkly stained by sin, he is thy brother yet!
Heir of the self-same heritage, child of the self-same God,
He hath but stumbled in the path thou hast in weakness trod.

Speak kindly to the erring, thou yet may'st lead them back,
With holy words and tones of love, from misery's thorny track;
Forget not, thou hast often sinned, and sinful yet may be,
Deal gently with the erring one, as God hath dealt with thee.

CHAPTER XVIII.

The Battle.

War must be
While men are what they are; while they have bad
Passions to be roused up; while ruled by men:
While all the powers and treasures of a land
Are at the beck of the ambitious crowd;
While injuries can be inflicted, or
Insults be offered; yea, while rights are worth
Maintaining, freedom keeping, or life having,
So long the sword shall shine: so long shall war
Continue, and the need of war remain.

A SLIGHT knowledge of history will enable any one to refute the assertion that "God is with the strongest army." No description of an encampment, was ever more vivid and touching than that of the opposing forces at Aphek, when Ben-hadad came with blustering words against Israel. "The children of Israel pitched before them like two little flocks of kids; but the Syrians filled the country." Yet the battle was not to the strong. One chased a thousand, and two put ten thousand to flight. We shall see it thus with King David.

Sir Robert Adair, the English ambassador, had

the pleasure of announcing to the Emperor of Russia, Alexander, the great defeat of the French at Vittoria. "By the help of Providence, sire," said he, "we have gained a great victory at Vittoria." "What!" said the emperor, "is Providence one of your allies?" "Yes, sire," replied the ambassador; "and the only one who requires no subsidies from us."

The king's forces were small compared with those of Absalom, but what they lacked in numbers was supplied by the justice of their cause. Joab was not the man to neglect his tactics. He seems to have chosen his ground so as to make the "wood of Ephraim" as advantageous as possible. By drawing them into it, and hemming them in, he, doubtless, was prepared to create a panic among the opposing troops. The mountaineers of Gilead with him knew how to make the best of a rough entangling forest. They were the Swiss of Bible times, kept in good training by their hos-. tile neighbours. The Bible says nothing of the lines, the columns, the right and left wings, nor the flankings, so fully detailed in modern accounts of battles. Josephus intimates that the rebel army made the attack, and that "upon the joining of the battle both sides showed great actions with their hands and their boldness: the one side exposing themselves to the greatest hazards and using their utmost alacrity, that David might recover his kingdom; the other being no way deficient, either in doing or suffering, that Absalom might not be deprived of that kingdom and brought to punishment by his father, for his impudent attempt against him." The rebels being the stronger in numbers, were solicitous not to be conquered by the few that were with Joab, for that would be the greatest disgrace to them; "while David's soldiers strove greatly to overcome so many ten thousands as the enemy had with them. Now David's men were conquerors, as superior in strength and skill in war; so they followed the others as they fled away through the forests and valleys."

Most likely Absalom's army was unwieldy and unworkable from its very size, and at the first shock gave way, was seized with a panic, fell into confusion, and ran in every direction, except toward their pursuers, "for the battle was then scattered over the face of all the country." Instead of a shelter, the forest proved a snare. God had foreseen this flight, and lest the routed army should again assemble, drill, organize more thoroughly, and prolong the contest, he had prepared the very ground for making speedy work of the rebellion. The bogs, jungles, and pitfalls, were all ready to receive them, and some think that wild beasts were at hand as a terrible reserve corps, to fulfil the designs of God in turning the victory to his servant David. "And the wood devoured more people that day than the sword devoured." There fell twenty thousand of the insurgents; most of them in the wilderness, where "thick oaks and tangled bushes, and thorny creepers growing over ragged rocks, and ruinous precipices down which the rebel army plunged in wild dismay, horses and men crushing each other to death in remediless ruin." Well does Bishop Hall write, "The God of armies, who at his pleasure can save with many or with few, takes part with justice, and lets Israel feel what it is to bear arms for an impious usurper. Let no man hope to prosper by rebellion; the very trees and thickets and pits and wild beasts of the woods shall conspire to the punishment of traitors."

It can hardly be that Absalom was last of all his army in holding his ground. No evidence of bravery has yet appeared in all his conduct. His sly, underhand intrigues, and his mean revenges the rather prove his cowardice. His irreverence and disobedience, his lawlessness and shameful willingness to run into sin, evince a total want of moral courage, and this is an important element in the bravery that can stand unflinching in battle. We should expect him to be among the loudest in boasting before the trying hour, and then the very first to break ranks and get out of danger. Riding on a mule he must have pressed the stupid animal to the utmost, and made better speed than many whom he had promised should reign with him, or he would die with them. Bewildered, unable to ride into the jungles, or over the rough ground of the wood, and bent upon some way of escape, he

seems to have brushed one wing of the loyal army,
and "met the servants of David." More terrified
than ever, and spurring his mule until anger made
him unmanageable, he was carried "under the
thick boughs of a great oak, and his head caught
hold of the oak,* and he was taken up between the
heaven and the earth; and the mule that was under him went away." Says Matthew Henry, "He
hung between heaven and earth, as unworthy of
either, as abandoned of both: earth would not
keep him, heaven would not take him." There must
be "no common fate for so uncommon a criminal.
God will here, as in the case of those other rebels,
Dathan and Abiram, 'create a new thing,' that it
may be understood how 'this man provoked the
Lord.'"

The beauty of Absalom became a curse to him
because he had perverted it. Men are often
brought to ruin by the gift or talent in which they
take a proud delight. "As if the even-handed justice of Heaven would have its perfect work, he fell
a victim to his ambition by means of that very personal adornment in which his vanity had so much
gloried." No doubt he was hung by his hair, for

---

* "I had a delightful ramble this morning in these grand old
forests, and now understand perfectly how Absalom could be caught
by the thick branches of an oak. The strong arms of these trees
spread out so near the ground, that one cannot walk erect beneath
them; and on a frightened mule, such a head of hair as that vain
but wicked son "polled every year, would certainly become inextri-
cably entangled." (*Land and the Book.*)

if by the neck, the sudden shock, or the close pressure of the branches, must have speedily killed him. But he lived long enough to have a world of thought pass swiftly through his mind, and to realize that with all the hearts he had stolen, there was not a friend near him in his final distress.

> O summer friendship,
> Whose flattering leaves, with the least gust drop off
> In the autumn of adversity!

A few days since we saw David threatened with sudden horrors. His sunshine friends left him to his fate. Yet as his darkness fell thicker, one star after another came forth, firm in their loyalty, and brave in their devotion to him. Few they were, but faithful. To them he appeared an old man, throneless, crownless, without treasures, without offices to bestow, without ability to reward their loyalty. But they stood the severe test. If he must be driven forth a wanderer hunted through forests, hiding in caves, with a price set upon his head, they would go with him, weep with him, bear his burdens, and stand between him and danger. Their fidelity cheered him. The voluntary devotion of strangers strengthened him. The Lord of Peniel stood by him. The angel of the Lord encamped around about him. And had the worst of disasters befallen him; had his troops been routed, and his cause been lost, there were warm and bold hearts which would not have deserted him in his extremity. They would have formed a wall around him, and with their lives defended his gray hairs.

Very strong is the contrast between his case and that of his son. Absalom had started out with court friends, gay admirers, flattered and fawning associates, men of stolen hearts, trimmers and traitors, a great and godless crew, who thought to be as desperately bold as pirates on a rough sea, but who would forsake their commander, and haste from the deck the moment the ship struck upon the rocks. And when calamity fell upon him, the prince was without a single friend. Not even an armour-bearer was with him as with Saul when he fled for Gilboa's refuge. In his flight he was alone. Some of his boastful company may have passed him as he hung in the oak, but not one had time to help him. Each was intent to save himself, and left him to the retribution which God had in reserve for him. Rarely was there a form of judgment more appropriate. . The great thief was utterly impoverished in his last hour. With all his havoc of loyal hearts, not one cleaves to him when he needs its aid. The traitor is betrayed. The heartless cruelty of the world in the hour of adversity is proverbial: "friendship that flames, goes out in a flash."

> The friends who in our sunshine live
> When winter comes are flown.

But never was there a more richly-deserved exhibition of it. Friends got without merit, go without mercy. An hour ago with untold warriors around him, Absalom claimed the throne, from which he would fling favours to the hungry crowd who helped him up its steps. But now he hangs utterly helpless, his only companion a conscience piercing his soul with arrows, and his only prospect a fearful looking-for of judgment. Had he hung there as long as we have dwelt upon this part of the divine retribution, he must have died, as Ahithophel and Judas did, by hanging. But he is to die by a " variety of deaths."

However Joab may have endeavoured to fire the hearts of his soldiers with unsparing vengeance, as if he would neutralize the tender charge of the king, there was one man who was cool enough to obey his superior, and who considered obedience the best loyalty. And still he knew that justice should be done, and who would do it? He told the general, as a soldier true to the cause, if not to the charge of his king. Joab, wondering that any man should not think David's command "more honoured in the breach than in the observance," chided him, " Why didst thou not smite him there to the ground? and I would have given thee ten shekels of silver and a girdle." Perhaps he had made such a promise to any one who should slay the prince. The reply proved him to be no hireling soldier : " Though I should receive a thousand shekels of silver in my hand, yet would I not put forth my hand against the king's son, for in our hearing the king charged thee and Abishai and Ittai, saying, "Beware that none touch the young man Absalom. Otherwise I should have wrought falsehood against mine own life, (and forfeited it by disobeying orders,) for there is no matter hid from the king, and thou thyself wouldst have set thyself against me." The giver of a bribe despises the man who receives it as a reward for violating law. Joab could not blame the soldier for his caution, and said, "I may not tarry thus with thee." It is no time for parleying and hanging on nice scruples. "The safety of the people is the supreme law."

It was the purpose of God that this rebel against him, his laws, his theocracy, and his anointed king, should perish. Providence has been against him. But it seems that for David's sake, he, in his tenderness, withheld the Almighty hand. He permitted a human agent to come to the execution. The instruments he employs for such stern judgments are commonly men of little compassion, of firm nerve, and of relentless purpose. Such a man was Joab. Pity was in his eyes a weakness, compassion an infirmity. No doubt, he regarded the king's gentleness as absurd, unjust to himself, and the kingdom. The usurper deserved to hurry over the last inch between him and death.

No slight token of the Divine hand in judgment is seen in the fact that Joab was once the best, the firmest, the boldest friend that Absalom had in all

19 *

Israel. His intercession had secured the recall of
the exile from Geshur. He had gone there and
brought him home. He had again become his advocate, and gained for him admittance to his father, the court, the city through which he paraded
in princely display, and the hearts of the people
whom he seduced from their allegiance. Of all
men the prince was most indebted to Joab. But
his offence grew rank, because he had plotted a
huge treason against the government which the
general served. Joab could forget that he had
once been the friend of a prince who had basely
forgotten that he was a son.

We must give Joab the credit of not having
burned with revenge, to take the prince's life with
his own hand, or else he would not have rebuked
the soldier for not doing it. It was not a deed that
he would care to boast of, or for which he would
receive any personal honours. Enough of such
deeds had been done by him already, and yet we
cannot credit him with any true repentance if we
look forward to his continued revenges. To classify
it with acts of regular warfare, he "took three darts
in his hand, and thrust them through the heart of
Absalom, while he was yet alive in the midst of the
oak. And ten young men that bare Joab's armour
compassed about and smote Absalom, and slew
him." They made sure his death. When one superior breaks his king's command, ten subordinates
imitate, and even go beyond, his example.

"There was, probably, a true regard for the king and kingdom in this act of Joab. He knew that Absalom could not with safety be suffered to live, and that it would be difficult to rid the state of so foul a member at any other time than now, when a just right to slay him had been earned in open battle. This is by no means to be classed with Joab's assassinations"—of Abner and Amasa. "It had nothing in common with them. Nothing can be alleged against him in this matter but his disobedience to the king; but he, in his position, felt that he dared to disobey him for his own good, and that he was quite prepared to vindicate and maintain this deed." (*Dr. Kitto.*) We must, however, be careful not to make the deed justify the man. That Absalom deserved death—even such a horrible death—for his rebellion, we cannot deny without doing violence to our just convictions. That God did not arrange the circumstances for this very mode of punishing the lawless, heartless, and rebellious prince, we cannot deny, for his hand is clearly seen. But yet the just deserts of Absalom, and the evident designs of God in visiting them upon him, do not alone justify the act. Though delivered of God to death, yet the actual slaying may have been by "wicked hands." Joab acted upon his own authority and by his own free will; God turned it to advantage in executing his purpose, and the doer must bear the entire responsibility for the deed.

Noble is the spirit of the general in the further strife. The people under his command are pursuing, slaying, and can scarcely be restrained. It is with them a soldier's work to be done in a soldier's way. But "he holds back the people." Enough has been done at the oak; it need not be extended through the forest. The nation's crime has been atoned by the death of its author. The rebels all deserve death, but mercy shall arrest the sword. "The generous heart can distinguish between the leader of a faction, and the misguided multitude, and can pity those who are deceived, while it ordains vengeance to their deceiver." Joab blew the trumpet for retreat, and the people returned from pursuing after Israel. And all Israel fled every man to his tent, or his home in his own tribe. They all went in haste, thinking and talking of how they might assure the king of their sudden conversion to loyalty, and be received again as good subjects of his government. None so base now in their estimation as Absalom, none so good as David. Their hearts are their own again, and to the rightful sovereign they shall be given.

From the Bible we derive authority and example for the solemn rites of burial. The dead, whoever they be, whatever they have done, are entitled to the ministries of kindness, and to a grave sacred and undisturbed. The guiltiest rebel may be buried with a pity for the lost, and a prayer for the living. It seems that Joab's men buried Absalom, and were not so true to a proper regard for the dead, or a tenderness for the feelings of the king. They could not separate the idea of his treason from his lifeless body. In their eyes it was still Absalom. "And they took Absalom, and cast him into a great pit in the wood, and laid a very great heap of stones upon him." Far grander was the burial which the ambitious young prince had planned for himself, as we shall see when considering his expectations of undying renown. He was cast into a pit, although he had reared for himself a pillar. Over him was a rude mound instead of his carefully-built monument.

If the busy Ahimaaz was as forward in battle as he wished to be in bearing the tidings, he must have been an eager soldier in the front rank, and given a hard chase to many a routed rebel, or a deadly blow to one entangled in the vines of the wood. He did not think "the first bringer of unwelcome news hath but a losing office." He imagined that the king would be glad to hear "how that the Lord had avenged him of his enemies." It was worthy of the high-priest's son to recognize the hand of God in the victory. But Joab restrained the officious and nimble-footed messenger. He feared to let the painful tidings go upon the wings of the wind, or by the tongue of one who might too bluntly break them to the king. The son of the high-priest would tell the whole truth, and that was what Joab wanted David not to know.

Another day would do as well, or if one must go,
let him be a more cautious and witty messenger.
Cushi was the man, better versed in the art of putting things in softer words. Scarcely was he out
of sight, when the eager Ahimaaz begged to run,
and at the third entreaty was allowed to go.
"Light of foot as a wild roe," he ran by the way
of the plain, and "seemed in running to devour the
way."

King David's heart had been for hours on the
rack, and the suspense became full of dread. He
was perhaps more anxious to learn that Absalom
lived, than that the battle was gained. It is a
touching picture—that of the king sitting between
the two gates, the watchman looking out from the
tower, calling to the porter, announcing the herald,
and preparing David to expect good news. If a
troop had been seen hurrying on in broken ranks,
it would have been a sign that Joab had been re-
pulsed, and in the panic, some of the terrified were
making good their escape. But "a man running
alone," must be a welcome courier. "Another
man running alone," was a still more gladly sight,
and especially as the foremost one was the son of
Zadok. Remembering his important message,
brought safely from Hushai, the king said, "He is
a good man, and cometh with good tidings." In
haste to relieve the king's mind, he cried out,
"Peace to thee—all is well." Coming nearer, he
fell down upon the earth, and said, "Blessed be

the Lord thy God, which hath delivered up the men that lifted up their hand against my lord the king." The victory was sure, but he told not the cost.

"Poor David is so much a father that he forgets he is a king, and therefore cannot rejoice in the victory." Made suspicious by the careful concealment of his son's name, he asks, "Is the young man Absalom safe?" In trying to be kind to his sovereign, the courier becomes false to the facts, replying, "When Joab sent the king's servant (Cushi), and me thy servant, I saw a great tumult, and knew not what it was." He may have seen such an unknown tumult, but he dishonestly evaded the truth. By suppressing the truth he suggests a falsehood. Cushi has studied his message, and, coming near, declares, "The Lord hath avenged thee this day of all them that rose up against thee." And then to the question, "Is the young man Absalom safe?" he replies with ingenious honesty, "The enemies of my lord the king, and all that rise up against thee to do thee hurt, be as that young man is." The whole truth is known, and the heart of the royal father breaks.

It has been thought that Joab wished to restrain the son of Zadok, lest the king should deal with the messenger of evil tidings as he had done with those who had brought him the news of the death of Saul and Ishbosheth. In order to save the young priest from such a fate, he sent Cushi, supposed to be an Ethiopian servant, whose loss would not be so great. If this be a happy guess at the truth, we have much to admire in the slow but wise courier. He earned the sparing of his life, even had there been the least danger. The truth should be told kindly to those who are scarcely able to bear it, but let there be evasion, no falsehood. Nor is Cushi the only one who put balm upon the sword that must pierce a parent's heart. When David's child was dead (2 Sam. xii. 18, 19) the servants hinted the fact in their whispering one to another, and the truth broke upon him, not as a thunder-clap, but as the gentle breaking of the day.

CHAPTER XIX.

O Absalom, my Son!

And the king was much moved, and went up to the chamber over the gate, and wept: and as he went, thus he said, O my son Absalom, my son, my son Absalom! would God I had died for thee, O Absalom, my son, my son!—2 Sam. xviii. 33.

IT is ever difficult to rebuke sorrow, and most of all when it seems unreasonable. Silence and sympathy may soothe, when arguments and reproofs only harrow up the heart. The one admirable thing in the conduct of Job's three mistaken friends was their sitting down with him seven days and speaking not a word unto him; for they saw that his grief was very great. Not until he spoke, did they break their silence, and then the man of wisest years and gentlest spirit began by saying, "If we assay to commune with thee wilt thou be grieved?"

There were none thus tender to weep with David when he needed comforters. To all about him his excessive grief seemed deserving of rebuke. He was ignoring the interests of the kingdom. He was forgetting that the rebel prince had doubly

20

forfeited his life, and attempted to take the life of his father. He was regardless of the victory, and the mercy of God, who had given it to his small army. He was abandoning himself to his natural feelings, and allowing himself to burst into wild, passionate cries, all the more painful to his attendants because in such contrast to his usually subdued emotions. In the agony of his private grief he was slighting the public welfare of the government. To their loyal hearts the government with its liberties, its religion and its laws, was worth more than life—unspeakably more than such a life as that of the lawless prince who had conspired against it. And now when the battle is gained, the kingdom recovered, the stolen crown won back by the sword, the danger passed, the rebellion crushed, he exclaims, "Would God I had died for thee, O Absalom!"

It would have been natural for all who heard this strange lamentation to meet it with the thought, "What if the king were dead! What if Absalom were conqueror!" Before their imaginations would come up the vision of terror. The Lord's anointed slain, and the usurper in power; the tyrant having his will and the ungodly having their way; religion put under the ban, and the floodgates of iniquity opened: loyal men, true to their king, cringing for the cold mercy of traitors, or treated with cruelty for a brave resistance to their burning rage; and the servants of God compelled to violate conscience and yield, or imperil their lives by refusing to submit to the rule of a graceless, lawless demagogue—all this, and more if the king's life and cause had been lost, and if Absalom had won the day and the throne. Surely, David did not mean all this, when he seemed to wish his life, worth ten thousand of theirs, laid down for a parricide, a murderer, and an armed rebel. But to the people it bore the tone of an utterance rash and unadvised.

We may hear in it the wail of a father, whose one all-absorbing grief renders him forgetful of the mighty interests of the nation, made dependent upon himself. If victory were not gained, if the government were not secured, and if the throne were not perfectly safe, he might have anxieties for these great national interests; but the very fact that he is sure of these, turns his whole attention to the fate of his son. He forgets Absalom's crafty intrigues, and forgets his cruelties toward his father, or rather he forgets the punishment they deserved, and which God has rendered, and thinks of the crimes that are unatoned, and their woes upon his son. His sins were great, but their very greatness rendered him all the more unfit for sudden death. While there was life, there was hope that in some way he might be reclaimed, redeemed, and brought to peace with his father and his God. But he is dead with all the guilt of a monstrous rebellion upon him. There is no hope in his death. He is gone from earth for ever; gone hopelessly beyond the reach of all the yearnings of a father's heart; gone where all the tears shed over him and the prayers offered for him can avail nothing, and this makes the tears fall faster, scalding a father's cheek; gone to answer for crimes that were revolting in the sight of God and men, and there seems no doubt but that the redemption of his soul has ceased for ever.

We may attribute to his grief this element of agony over a lost soul—the lost soul of a beloved son. It is the most generous view to be taken of his sorrow, and then how noble it appears! He would die for Absalom, if that could redeem him from his guilty death. There are parents now who know something of what this means. It is the most painful and unselfish sorrow that a godly father or mother can know. With it nothing else can be named in comparison.

A group of friends were once talking together of their troubles. One spoke of a loss, another of a bereavement, but at last one sad, pale woman said with plaintive voice, "Not one of you know what trouble is." She then drew the picture of a southern home where the years rolled by uncounted, and a happy family sang and smiled in bliss. But one night, said she, "one of those fierce black storms came on, when the rains poured down incessantly. Morning dawned, and still the elements raved. The whole Savannah seemed afloat with wrecks. The little stream near our dwelling became a raging torrent. Before we were aware of it our house was surrounded with water. I took my infant and sought a place of safety, while my husband and sons strove to save what they could of our property. At last a fearful surge swept away my husband, and he never rose again. No one loved a husband more, but *that was not trouble.*

"The sullen river raged around the huge trees, dead branches, logs, wrecks of houses, drowning cattle, masses of rubbish went floating by. I saw my boys—they waved their hands, and pointed upward. I knew the farewell signal, and you, mothers, cannot imagine my anguish. I saw them perish, and yet, *that was not trouble.*

"I pressed my child close to my heart, and when the water rose to my feet, I climbed into the low branches of a tree, and so was kept until an All-powerful Hand stayed the waves, and I was saved. All my earthly possessions were gone, all my earthly hopes were blighted, yet *that was not trouble.*

"That child was all I had left on earth. I laboured night and day to support him and myself, and sought to train him in the right way; but as he grew older, evil companions won him away from me. He ceased to care for his mother's counsels; he would sneer at her entreaties and agonizing prayers. He left my humble roof that he might be unrestrained in the pursuit of evil; and at last,

20 *

when heated by wine one night, he took the life of a fellow-being, and ended his own upon the scaffold. My heavenly Father had filled my cup of sorrow before, but now it ran over. *That was trouble*, such as I hope God in his mercy may ever spare you." She might have exclaimed, "Would God I had died for thee, O my son, my son!"

And now notice how patiently and profitably King David took rebuke. The people were sorry that "he was grieved for his son," when they thought he ought to be satisfied, or at least submissive. He was a father, and they would treat with delicate tenderness his unquenched affection and boundless distress. The king was aged, worn, and greatly burdened, and they were exceedingly careful not to offend him in his sorrow. They did not march from the battle field as conquerors with their ranks preserved, with the spoils of war, with trophies wrested from the dying, and with the shouts of triumph. But they "gat them by stealth, that day, into the city, as people being ashamed steal away when they flee in battle." They may have done this rather from policy than in real sympathy, as if they had been so advised by the crafty Joab, and said, "As the king wishes Absalom were alive, we will disguise our victory, and act as if he had beaten us, and driven us in shame and fear into the city. Then the king may bethink himself of what he is wishing, and come to know what a great and good victory we have gained for him by the help of God. He may then turn his tears into thanks because his army is not so defeated as it appears." But David was not affected by a disguise so boldly in contrast with the reality. The sight of his servants reminded him more painfully of the absence and death of his son, and he covered his face, and cried with a loud voice "O my son Absalom; O Absalom, my son, my son!"

Joab was tried beyond all his patience, and he resolved to put an end to a grief in his eyes unworthy and unpardonable. He was not serving his king for naught, nor did the brave soldiers deserve such a slight put upon their courage and their triumph. They would not bear it. If their services were not appreciated, they would leave him to his grief and ingratitude. A king who could not pay bounties to his brave defenders ought, at least, to give them thanks, and the most foolish thing for him to do, would be to ignore their victory. Joab, like the first Napoleon, had the gift of eloquence, and his speech to the king proves his faithfulness to the government at an hour when its largest interests were at stake. If too blunt as an orator, he was not too zealous as a general, in his thrilling speech.

" Thou hast shamed this day the faces of all thy servants, which this day have saved thy life, (when Absalom sought it,) and the lives of thy sons, and of thy daughters, and of thy wives, and of thy concubines, in that thou lovest thine enemies and hatest thy friends. For thou hast declared this day (by thy untimely grief) that thou regardest neither princes nor servants; for this day, I perceive, that if Absalom had lived, and all we had died this day, then it had pleased thee well. Now therefore, arise, go forth, and speak comfortably unto thy servants, for I swear by the Lord, if thou go not forth, there will not tarry one with thee this night; and that will be worse unto thee than all the evil that befell thee from thy youth until now."

Thus thrilled and threatened the king came to himself, shook off his grief, no longer appeared unto men to mourn, and went to the gate which served as the public hall of the city. There he sat to smile upon his troops when they should present themselves, welcome them and thank them for their services and their successes. Men are willing to be commanded, if they may be also commended when they are faithful. The people heard of the king's public appearance, came before him, and the mourning was turned into an acknowledgment of the victory.

The oft-quoted poem of a living author, represents the body of Absalom brought before the king, when he bends over it, and utters his unavailing lament. The facts are not at all consistent with such a fancy. Absalom's body had already been disposed of, and there is no shadow of probability that the king attempted to recover it. When imagination does violence to the Scripture narrative, the poetry is spoiled, and the truth sacrificed. The entire poem is so untrue to fact and real feeling that it deserves rebuke. The simple record rebukes it, for there is nothing in it like the unparalleled description of the king weeping as he went up to his chamber, and losing himself in the emotions of grief. But God wiped away all tears from his eyes.

CHAPTER XX.

The Pillar in the King's Dale.

"The noblest renown is posthumous fame, and the most refined ambition is the desire of such fame."—JAMES HAMILTON, D. D.

WERE it not for one verse, we should not know that Absalom had a little refinement in his ambition, and wished for something beyond the revellings of a day or the follies of a life. We should think of him as too absorbed in mirth ever to plan a monument. To us he would appear as one so entirely given to foppery, feasting and the use of power for temporary advantage, as to live by the common oriental motto, "let us eat and drink, for to-morrow we die:" or as one playing the demagogue for an office that would enlarge the sphere of his baser passions, and rebelling, for rebellion's sake, against all that would secure to his name a happy remembrance. We should regard him as altogether thoughtless of death, of a grave, and of the good opinions of the after generations. But if he cared not what men thought of his conduct, he did care what should be the fate of his name.

It must be remembered after his death. He took pains to secure a posthumous fame. One verse tells it, and the place of that verse in the Bible is remarkable. Just after the record of his burial, as if to mark emphatically the contrast between the disgrace he received and the honour he had anticipated, we read thus: "Now Absalom in his lifetime had taken and reared up for himself a pillar, which is in the king's dale: for he said, I have no son* to keep my name in remembrance: and he called the pillar after his own name: and it is called unto this day Absalom's place."

Early then he took this matter in hand: very likely in the days when he gave more time to hairdressers than to the teachers of wisdom. How ridiculous for a young man of twenty to rear such a monument! To reduce the absurdity a little it has been supposed that he undertook the glorious enterprise about the time that he indulged in horses, chariots and his fifty outrunners. If so, his two sons were then dead, and his loss ought to have led him to think of their graves, rather than of a pillar of renown for himself. It ought to have sobered him so that he would have set about rearing a character for himself, and doing something worthy of remembrance. An example of repentance and of holiness would have consecrated his

* "I do not wonder that it was thought a great misfortune to die childless in old time when they had not fuller light—it seems so completely wiping a man out of existence."—*Life of Thomas Arnold.*

name on the roll of the saints. Perhaps, like
Aaron Burr, he bestowed the proudest attentions
upon his beautiful daughter Tamar, and what a
blessed memory he might have attained had he
taught her in the ways of the Lord!

Her children might have risen up to call him
blessed, and in his old age buried him in a nobler
tomb than any his own hands could prepare. And
if she was the mother or grandmother of Abijam,
it might not have been said of him, that he walked
in all the sins of his father Rehoboam. Or had
Absalom not wasted his money upon dress and
equipage, and bestowed it upon the poor, his alms
might have come up as a memorial before God.
A loaf of bread put upon the table of a serf would
have been a better monument than a marble pillar
in the king's dale.

> His kindness would have embalmed his name;
> Goodness, not greatness, would have been his fame.

But he was bent upon a wicked, cruel, and rebellious career which would set him among the execrated
of mankind, and the name Absalom sounded so
musically in his ear, that he imagined its tone
would bring all the discords of his life into har-
mony. If the pen of wisdom would not transmit
it, if the trump of war would not sound it forth, or
if the anecdotes of brilliant wit would never em-
blazon it, he would write it on the chiselled rock.
His must be a pillar extraordinary, imposing in

the distance and towering loftily above the tombs of good and holy men whose names would never die, because their works should follow them. "It would be injustice to mankind if he suffered the memory of his grandeur to perish," and he could not afford to trust it to the uncertainties of his own merits, or of the people's gratitude. "His care was to have his name kept in remembrance, and it is so, to his everlasting dishonour. He could not be content in the obscurity of the rest of David's sons, but would be famous, and is therefore justly made forever infamous."—(*Henry.*)

His very ambition for renown was made to mock his memory, for he was buried in disgrace, far from his pillar, in a pit. He received a traitor's ancient burial. The heap of stones was not raised over him in honour because he was the king's son, but in detestation of his enormous crime. He was deemed worthy of the punishment due to a rebellious son, (Deut. xxi. 18–21,) who was to be led outside of the city walls and stoned to death. Jewish writers say that this sentence was not actually inflicted, but by casting stones over the grave, the people showed that it ought to have been. They also say that every passer-by was accustomed to throw a stone on the heap that covered the remains of Absalom, and as he threw it he said, "Cursed be the memory of rebellious Absalom, and cursed for ever be all wicked children that rise up in rebellion against their parents." In "The

21

Land and the Book," the author writes, "It is a wide-spread custom for each one as he passes the spot where any notorious murderer has been buried, to cast a stone upon it. I have often seen this done, and yielding to the popular indignation have thrown my stone among the rest. I am reminded of all this"—the case of Absalom—"by the conduct of my guide, who has actually dismounted to spit upon this heap, and add his pebble to the growing pile."

None but the vainest self-conceited fool would commemorate a victory before he had won it. Yet perhaps Absalom did. The tradition is that his monument was pointed with a hand, the symbol of power and of victory. Such pillars were in ancient use, and are still found in the East. Josephus says that the prince named his pillar, "Absalom's Hand," and such is the Hebrew word rendered in our version, "Absalom's Place." The deserved interpretation of the symbol, if he put it there, was that his hand was raised against heaven, and against all thrones of God and men.

The pillar lasted its time, but crumbled at length. Another rose on the supposed spot, not in honour of Absalom, but from an eagerness to restore fallen monuments. It still stands in the valley of Jehoshaphat, and " cannot be less than forty feet high." The natives believe it to be Absalom's tomb, and spit at it, and throw stones against it as they pass by, hating the ancient rebel whose name they remember. "He need not have reared a pillar in the king's dale: his name will long survive his monument, and stand as a warning to all young men, to tell the story of the worst of sons, the prince of demagogues, the fallen victim of a vaulting ambition."

Looking from this monument to the death, the disgrace, and the lasting infamy of the man who reared it, let us quote the words of Chrysostom, from a sermon which would have been appropriate in Jerusalem if Nathan the prophet had preached them at the funeral of the prince, and may not yet have lost their point. "Where is now the feast of joyous assemblies? Where are the crowns and magnificent ornaments? Where the flattering reports of the city—the acclamations of the circus— the adulations of thousands of spectators? All have passed away! The wind by one blast has swept the leaves, and now they show to us a dead tree, torn from its roots—so violent has been the tempest. It lies a broken ruin. Where are the pretended friends—the swarm of parasites—the tables charged with luxury—the wine circulated during entire days—where the various refinements of feasting—the supple language of slaves? What has become of them all? A dream of the night which vanishes with the day! A flower of spring which fades in the summer!—a shade which passes!—a vapour which scatters!—a bubble of water which bursts!—a spider's web which is torn! 'Vanity

of vanities, all is vanity.' Inscribe these words on
your walls, on your vestments, on your palaces, on
your streets, on your houses, on your windows, on
your doors ; inscribe them on your consciences, in
order that they may represent it incessantly to
your thoughts.   Repeat them in the morning;
repeat in the evening; and in the assemblies of
fashion, let each repeat to his neighbour, " Vanity
of vanities, all is vanity.' "

The only posthumous fame that can outlast all
time, and extend through eternity, is the memory
of God.   The only deathless names are those written in the Lamb's book of life.   Humble men and
women they may be ; the Marys, the Dorcases,
the fishermen of Galilee, or even the unnamed fel-
low-labourers of the Apostle Paul.   Mary did a
little thing when she anointed Jesus' feet, but
" wheresoever this gospel shall be preached throughout the whole world, this also that she hath done,
shall be spoken of for a memorial of her."   Great
deeds have been forgotten, great names have no
living record, marble monuments have crumbled
into dust, but Mary—

> " Thou hast thy record in the monarch's hall,
> And on the waters of the far mid sea;
> And where the mighty mountain shadows fall,
> The Alpine hamlet keeps a thought of thee :
> Where'er, beneath some oriental tree,
> The Christian traveller rests—where'er the child
> Looks upward from the pious mother's knee

There art thou known: where'er the book of light
Bears hope and healing, there beyond all blight
Is borne thy memory, and all praise above:
O say, what deed so lifted thy sweet name,
Mary, to that pure silent place of fame?
One lowly offering of exceeding love."

21 *

CHAPTER XXl.

The Restoration.

O happy kings
Whose thrones are raised in their subjects' hearts.

NEVER did a rebellion sooner come to an end than that of Absalom. The people had gone into it with stolen, not with earnest hearts. After being defeated, they were, at once, disgusted with the whole affair, and fled home in haste, to avoid the suspicion that they had ever been such fools as to engage in a conspiracy, doomed to wreck from the first. Nor did they hide away in a corner, to wait until the king's wrath should be turned from them, but zealously set to work to pave the way for his restoration. In this the tribes of Israel (not including Judah) were the most forward. There was now no man like David, and they called to remembrance his prowess and fatherly care, saying, " The king saved us out of the hand of our enemies, and he delivered us out of the hand of the Philistines ; and now he is fled out of the land for Absalom. And Absalom, whom we anointed king over us, is dead in battle. Now, therefore, why speak ye not a word of bringing the king back?" So great a benefactor should not remain in banishment. "Note, good services done to the public, though they may be forgotten for a while, yet will be remembered again, when men come to their right minds." The strife among them was, probably, not whether the king should be invited back, for in this they were agreed: but why was it not more speedily done? Whose fault was the delay? "The people laid the blame on the elders, and the elders on the people, and one tribe on another." The noise of the goodly strife reached the king, and must have pleased him, while remaining in his quarters at Mahanaim.

After the sudden dispersion of the rebel army, David had the choice of two courses: either to march to Jerusalem at the head of his victorious troops and take military possession of the capital, or to wait until the people should invite him back to the throne from which they had driven him. The first plan would have been too hasty. It might not have secured the bringing back of the stolen hearts. By the second plan, he would make no show of force in claiming his rights, and thus avoid what is always unpopular. When the tribes felt their need of a king, they would hail his restoration, and the Philistines might cause them to need him very soon. His delicacy and wise management are highly commendable. He had reason to

expect that Judah would first move in the matter.
Was Amasa, the defeated rebel general, keeping
back David's own tribe? The hint is not unjust,
(chap. xix. 13.) But while chagrined at the cold-
ness of Judah, he is cheered by the warmth of the
ten tribes of Israel.

What he feared was disunion. Already were
the party lines drawn between Israel and Judah.
He must not be restored by only one party, and to
rouse up Judah he sent Zadok and Abiathar the
priests, with an affectionate entreaty. If they
hung back, through fear that David would make
an example of them, because among them the rebellion had first been organized, they should be
assured of the kindest treatment. The past should
be forgotten, and he would assume the office of
shepherd and father of his people. The message
to them indicated his policy toward the insurgents;
"Why are ye the last to bring the king back to
his house? seeing the speech of all Israel is come
to the king, even to his house. Ye are my brethren, ye are my bones and my flesh; wherefore,
then, are ye the last to bring back the king? And
say ye to Amasa, Art thou not of my bone, and
of my flesh? God do so to me, and more also, if
thou be not captain of the host before me con-
tinually in the room of Joab."

No vengeance, then, was to be taken on the rebels, and the leader of their forces was not only to
be spared from a traitor's deserts, but even pro-

moted to the highest military office. Comfortable news, certainly, and the people were overpowered by the goodness and generosity of the aged king. He was the same fatherly David that he had ever been, willing and anxious to forgive his rebellious sons. The preachers of mercy are the most successful. David thus "bowed the heart of the men of Judah, even as the heart of one man, so that they sent back this word to the king, Return thou, and all thy servants."

From one extreme they rushed into another. The last to speak for David, they were the first to act for him. Such was their haste that they increased the very danger of disunion that the king had dreaded. Their leading men came to Gilgal, met the king, and without waiting for their jealous rivals in the ten tribes, they prepared to conduct him over Jordan.

On the banks were certain others who were moving on their own responsibility, because they had selfish reasons for securing the good graces of the king. None were likely to be more officious in kind assistance, pushing themselves forward to row the ferry-boats in which were borne the king and his household.

Scarcely had the royal feet touched the soil, when the best of friends were ready with their greetings, when Shimei made a better use of the tongue that had lately cursed David, and of the dust that he had cast into the air in derision.

Falling down he sought to agree with his adversary quickly while in the way with him. Even the cursing coward has boldness now to cringe before the man of mercy, for he knows there is no danger. He has tried to commend himself by starting the first of his tribe, coming in the goodly company of Judah; and bringing with him a thousand men of Benjamin. His confession and plea show him to be more crafty than contrite. "Let not my lord impute iniquity unto me, neither do thou remember that which thy servant did perversely the day that my lord the king went out of Jerusalem, that the king should take it to his heart. For thy servant doth know that I have sinned; therefore, (in my repentance,) I am come the first this day of all the house of Joseph, to go down to meet my lord the king." Abishai thought that he should be made to kiss the dust in death, but David felt, more than ever that the sons of Zeruiah were too hard for him, and by an oath sealed his pardon. We shall find that David afterward, considered this matter, and on the principle that a wrong promise is better broken than kept, broke the seal of pardon, and gave the death-warrant for Shimei's execution. (1 Kings ii. 8, 9.)

Ziba also had good cause for making an early appearance, and to render it more imposing brought his fifteen sons and twenty servants along with him. If the king saw what a large family he had to support, pity for them might keep him from entirely depriving Ziba of the property which he had obtained in so rascally a manner. Even swindlers must live. This one knew that the less he said the better, for his slow but sure master was on the way to Jerusalem to lay his case before the king. And here we may notice the visit of Mephibosheth, the son (of Jonathan, the son) of Saul. So strong had been his loyalty that he "had neither dressed his feet, nor trimmed his beard, nor washed his clothes, from the day that the king departed, until the day he came again in peace"—thus dooming himself to hardships similar to those of his sovereign. Not yet had David any clue to the late affair of Ziba, and thinking that of all men whom he had ever favoured, the son of Jonathan was the very last to desert him, he put the stern question, " Wherefore wentest not thou with me, Mephibosheth? And he answered, My lord, O king, my servant deceived me; for thy servant said, I will saddle me an ass, that I may ride thereon, and go to the king: because thy servant is lame. And he hath slandered thy servant unto my lord, the king; but my lord the king is as an angel of God ; do therefore what is good in thine eyes. For all of my father's house were but dead men before my lord the king; yet didst thou set thy servant among them that did eat at thine own table. What right therefore have I to cry any more unto the king?" One never likes to admit that he cannot read human nature, and has been deceived; and David was scarcely willing to acknowledge that he was grossly duped when he confiscated the lame man's estate. The case was perplexing, for even Mephibosheth might be deceiving him. His reply was something less than generous. "Why speakest thou any more of thy matters? I have said, Thou and Ziba divide the land." This seems unjust. One or the other deserved the entire property. If Ziba had told the truth, he should have all; if a lie, then none. "The matter however is not so bad as it looks. The king reverts to what he had said, which carries the mind back to the first arrangement, which was that Mephibosheth should be proprietor, and Ziba his tenant, dividing the *produce* of the land between them.

"It may be, therefore, that the king meant to be understood as restoring this arrangement—thus depriving Ziba of the advantage which his treachery acquired, without ejecting him from his tenancy under Mephibosheth. Even this would be hard enough for the son of Jonathan to be thus still connected with a steward who had betrayed him. But the student of history knows that at a restoration, the rules of right and wrong are seldom strictly carried out, and the king having two parties to satisfy, feels obliged to act upon compromises, which give to all something less than their due."—(*Kitto.*)

We are disarmed of all suspicion toward Mephibosheth, by his noble reply. "Yea, let him take

all, forasmuch as my lord the king is come again
in peace unto his own house." This loyal man
was afterwards spared by David, when the Gibeon-
ites took a savage vengeance upon the house of
Saul, for injuries received when he was king. (2
Sam. xxi. 7.)

Social convulsions bring to light the characters
of men. Not a few, long honoured, are found to
be hollow-hearted; others, hidden in a corner, are
found to be patriots of the noblest stamp. Barzillai was the man to partly fill the void in David's
heart. Being a "very great man" he had helped
to store the commissary department. As a "very
aged man, even fourscore years old," his sympathies were most refreshing to the king, when young
Israel was in rebellion. He came to give his last
lift in aiding David over the river. To have such
a noble specimen of loyal humanity at the court
would make the king's heart immensely rich, and
he said to the good old chieftain, "Come thou over
with me, and I will feed thee with me in Jerusalem." But he was "too old a tree to be trans-
planted." The feasting and the singing would be
no delight. And just like such a man, who mo-
destly counts himself as nothing, he thinks that he
has been a burden to the king even in his kindness, and why be a burden any longer? If permitted the favour, he "will go a little way over
Jordan with the king," and then he must turn
back, die in his own city, and be laid by the grave

22

of his father and his mother. He had honoured them while they lived, and his days had been long in the land. "How long have I to live?" He was thinking of another world, and perhaps, of the meeting with David when nothing should part them for ever. He sent his servant with the king, received his kiss and his blessing, and returned to his own home.

"Behold, how great a matter a little fire kindleth." Once a miller and his apprentice quarrelled about wages; others took part in it; the whole town became divided; then the nation took it up, or rather took up the weightier matters growing out of it; then nearly all France and Germany were involved in the "miller's war," and years passed before it was settled. A mere point of etiquette, violated, set on flame the jealousy between Israel and Judah. The avalanche had long been gathering, and the shouts of rejoicing put it in motion. Judah did not wait at the Jordan for the brother-tribes to appear, and take part in helping David over the river. It was a dignified proceeding, and surely, ought to have been done by a committee of all the tribes! But lo! in their officious haste, "the people of Judah conducted the king, and also half the people of Israel." The other half of Israel are slighted, and mortally offended. The unceremonious affair has been as secret as a theft, and they will not endure the insult of being neglected. Judah has assumed too

much in claiming the right and the honour of restoring the king as if he belonged especially to
them by right of monopoly. And now Israel
cares less for the king than about this point of
ceremony. A hot contention arises between the
two parties. At first it is quite enough to amuse
the king to see each contending for the best right
to bring back the sovereign whom they had united
in driving from the throne. The men of Israel
ask him, "Why have our brethren, the men of
Judah, stolen thee away?" Before he can reply
the men of Judah answer, quite unwisely, "Because the king is near of kin to us: wherefore
then should ye be angry for this matter? have we
eaten at all of the king's cost? (have we been
feasting before you could come?) or hath he given
us any gift?" To be called angry provokes yet
more their rage, and the Israel-party set up a still
higher claim. "We have ten parts in the king,
and we have also more right in David than ye:
why then did ye despise us, that our advice should
not be first had in bringing back our king?" Men
often assume to be cool in a quarrel in order to
cloak their anger, and thus "the words of the men
of Judah were fiercer than the words of the men
of Israel."

As Dr. Chalmers remarks, "Here was a fester-
ment that broke out at a future day," and even
now, "came to a formidable eruption." There
happened to be present a schemer of Absalom's

school of politics, a man of Belial, named Sheba, a Benjaminite, and he thought that the tide of his fortune had come. As a leader was wanted, he put himself forward, and hoped to persuade those who claimed "ten parts in the king," that they had really no part at all. Blowing a trumpet he raised the seditious cry, "We have no part in David, neither have we inheritance in the son of Jesse: every man to his tents, O Israel." It was enough. The standard of revolt was raised, and every man of Israel seceded, and followed the new demagogue. The king was left to his tribal kindred, who saw him safely restored to his city, palace, and throne.

CHAPTER XXII.

Imitators of Absalom.

Vengeance is still alive: from her dark covert
She stalks in view.

THE most abundant materials had been prepared
by Absalom, the fire was kindled by letting fall a
careless spark, and now a vast spreading confla-
gration must be put out by pouring blood upon it.
The king must teach those who had declared that they
had no longer ten parts in David, that he had ten
parts in Israel.   It was painful to find one trouble
rising out of another: deep was calling unto deep:
the sword was not yet departed from his house.
Much sooner than he expected, he had cause to
test the generalship of his nephew Amasa.   He
ordered him to issue a call for the troops of Judah
to assemble within three days.   He set about it,
but the three days passed, and no warriors were
mustered before the king.   The rapid Joab would
hardly have required even this short time, and no
doubt David began to see his error in relieving him
of the chief command.   For his rough faithfulness

22 *

to his king in finishing Absalom and his rebellion,
David had regarded him with abhorrence. His removal was not a popular act, as was now proved,
for the people were unwilling to follow the new
leader, so lately the rebel commander, and now
chief by the gift of an office. David himself was
quick in military operations, and long used to
Joab's driving style, and he could not brook
Amasa's delay. Without giving him a day of
grace, and fearing that Sheba would do more harm
than Absalom did, he sent Abishai upon the march
with the home-guards, foreign troops, Joab's veterans, and such mighty men as the hour could afford. Joab was not the man to stand silent as
"vengeance leaning on a lance." He was not to
be outdone, nor put out by a slight. In spite of
his disgrace he joined the army. He thought that
to make a good peace, there must be a good war,
and as for the war he must make it. Besides, he
had an affair of jealousy and revenge to settle.
He probably became the actual commander. At
Gibeon they halted, and Amasa overtook them
with his recruits. Joab went to meet him, and so
contrived that his sword should drop from its sheath
as he came near. It seemed to his new rival as an
accident, and Joab, snatching it up, made himself
so polite that he excited no suspicion, by holding it
in his hand. Taking Amasa by the beard to kiss
him, and asking, "Art thou in health, my brother?"
he buried the naked blade in his body under the

fifth rib, very much as he had done with Abner. It was a bold atrocious deed—nothing less than the decided murder of a general in command.

One of Joab's men then shouted out, "He that favoureth Joab, and he that is for David, let him go after Joab" to the battle. When the corpse of Amasa was removed out of the highway his troops obeyed the call. There was magic in the name, and confidence in the war-tried general, so that the number of his forces greatly increased on the march. The rebel leader after rambling about and failing to gather the tribes as he expected, shut himself up in the fortified town of Abel-Beth-Maachah. Joab besieged it, battered the wall, and made ready for a general storm. One woman by her wisdom saved the city. "We may suppose it was the first time he had ever treated with a woman in martial affairs." She tells him, (for so reads the marginal version of chapter xx. 18,) that the elders of the city had said in the beginning of the siege, "Surely they will ask of the dwellers in Abel that the traitor be given up, and thus end the matter." The hint is taken, and Joab declares "Only deliver him up, and I will depart from the city." She promises that his head shall be thrown over the wall, goes to "the people in her wisdom," and persuades them to execute the rebel chief. They do it, fling his head to Joab, and thus prove that "wisdom is better than strength." The trump is blown, the loyal forces retire, are dis-

banded and every man goes to his tent or house.
"And Joab returned to Jerusalem unto the king,"
having proved, he probably thought, that David
could never do without him. So far as a complete
and brilliant success could compensate for his
crime, he had done the best possible. He had
won back the lost command, and, as he was too
great to be displaced, he was permitted to keep it.
David was not always his own master; Joab was
really often above him, doing great service by his
rough patriotism and ready valour, but injuring
the good name of the king, and the moral reputation of his government, by actions which David de-
tested in his inmost soul. The one thing he could
do was to make short work of a rebellion.

Perhaps we may be tempted to make his heroism
and loyalty excuse, if not atone for, his great
crimes. We forget the private sins of such a man
when so covered by public services. But David
could not forget them. To him Joab was as one
of the sons of Belial, who were as thorns that must
be rooted out and thrust away, and yet "cannot
be taken with hands, but the man that shall touch
them must be fenced with iron, and the staff of a
spear," that he may toss them into the fire. (2
Samuel xxiii. 6, 7.) It was hard to bring to justice the great general who had never lost an important battle, and who had rendered the king
more vigorous service than any other man in the
kingdom. David postponed the trying matter to

the last moment of the eleventh hour, and from his death-bed threw off the burden from his conscience. Joab was old, but he must account for his old sins. He could not but notice that "Joab had turned after Adonijah, though he turned not after Absalom." He was forced to consider the consequences to the realm if these crimson sins of Joab were suffered longer to pass unpunished, and there was good ground on which to bring him to justice.

The reason expressly given was the murders of Abner and Amasa, "Whom he slew, and shed the blood of war in (a time of) peace, and put the blood of war upon his girdle that was about his loins, and in his shoes that were upon his feet." David had forgiven and made peace with these rebellious men just before Joab murdered them, and this was setting himself above his king. Here the words "what Joab did to me,"—trampling upon my authority and despising my amnesty—may have their meaning. "Do therefore according to thy wisdom, and let not his hoar head go down to the grave in peace." He was put to death at the altar and was buried in his own house in the wilderness.

In retiring from the field of blood over which we have been walking, lessons enough crowd upon us. The sin of rebellion has written its warnings in crimson, and against it stand forever the monuments raised by Divine justice. What a list of rebels! Ish-bosheth, and Abner, Absalom, Ahithophel and Amasa, Shimei and Sheba, and at the last even Adonijah and Joab are in revolt. They all perished by a death which their treason brought upon them. The earthly pardon granted to some of them could not ward off the judgment of God. And how contagious is the sin of disobedience and revolt! Absalom draws "all Israel" after him. Nor does his death or the dispersion of his army end the iniquity. The malaria is not driven from the towns and valleys of Palestine. The canker eats again at the national heart. The tribes quarrel, draw party lines, and finally are for ever separated by the revolt of the ten tribes, who become so utterly extinguished that their doom is a mystery on which no light is cast by all the researches of history. There are national sins which bring enlightened nations under calamities, and may sink them into oblivion, and one of them is rebellion against a righteous government.

Sinful as this is, there is something worse. To refuse obedience to God is worse, for it is the most enormous revolt possible for men. Human authorities may overlook this crime; it lies not in their sphere, or within their jurisdiction, but God will bring the guilty to punishment, unless they accept his abundant pardon. No public services to a human government can remove the guilt of this sin. Amasa had put himself in revolt against God, and however David might pardon, or he serve his forgiving king, yet on him the blow of justice must fall for his sins against Jehovah. Still stronger is the case of Joab. His national services could not compensate for his crimes against the Lord. Nor can any of our patriotic deeds and sacrifices obliterate the penalty written by God upon our personal sins. Honour the loyal man, who like good old Barzillai bestowed his largest gererosities to his country's defenders; honour the hidden ones, who like Mephibosheth patiently suffer losses, rather than have any complicity with rebellion, or make disturbances which will weaken the rightful power of an administration; honour the soldiers, who put their lives in jeopardy on every battle-field, or fall a sacrifice to victory, but resist the temptation to believe that services and sacrifices paid to any human government will atone for personal sins against God. It may be pleasing to think it, the notion may be popular, and is in our times, but the noblest patriotism cannot secure the salvation of the soul. A patriotic man, a brave soldier, may swear profanely, as we know most painfully by our ears, but "the Lord will not hold him guiltless that taketh his name in vain." A loyal man may be grossly intemperate, as we know most mournfully by our eyes, but the Lord hath written, "No drunkard shall inherit the kingdom of heaven." Tell the soldier, who goes from your homes, of the earthly glory which the brave and the dying patriot may win; tell him that duty is a far higher motive than dreams of glory, but do not deceive his soul by whispering that bravery will gain for him the infinite rewards of heaven. True to the last, he may be, to his government, but untrue from the first, he may have been to his God, and to the Saviour who shed his blood to redeem him. Commend to him the example of a young recruit, who in serving his country wished to serve his God. Before taking the oath of allegiance to the government, he vowed allegiance to King Jesus, made the profession of his faith, was baptized, and enrolled among the people of God. He could "endure hardness as a good soldier of Jesus Christ," and march with a steadier courage to the battle. No less a Christian he was all the more a patriot.

Nor can any mere moral services and sacrifices in the moral kingdom save the soul. Good works may be the very best that we can render, but they cannot buy off the penalty due to our sins. The sins may be older than the works, and, like the crimes of Joab, must remain against us until we accept a relief from their penalties through Christ. If we have fled for refuge to the cross of Jesus, and there be any tempter that bids us away, that he may deceive us into death, we each may say with firmest faith, "Nay, but I will die here." And dying there we may hear the words, "To-day shalt thou be with me in Paradise."